Praise for *Praying for You*

"Faced with parenting challenges and c
David and Mercedes Rizzo to be your mentors and companions along
your family's spiritual journey. Filled with practical wisdom and experienced perspective, *Praying for Your Special Needs Child* is the perfect
resource for the parent, guardian, teacher, family member, or friend of a
child with special needs."

—Lisa M. Hendey, founder of CatholicMom.com
and author of *The Grace of Yes*

"Parents of children with disabilities face unique challenges. In my work
as a child and family psychologist, I have often sat with parents as they
alternatively expressed loneliness, exhaustion, hopefulness, desperation,
and joy in small successes. Drawing from their own experience as parents
of a child with autism, David and Mercedes Rizzo offer an honest and
insightful guide for parents of children who are differently-abled. This
straightforward and practical book will help parents know they aren't
alone. It will navigate parents through frustration, fear, and confusion,
and guide them as they pray for wisdom, protection, patience and grace.
This book is a tremendous gift to parents of children with disabilities and
to church leaders who provide them with welcome and pastoral care."

—Dr. Joseph White, clinical child psychologist and national catechetical
consultant for Our Sunday Visitor Publishing and Curriculum

"Many of us are familiar with the myriad of inspiring books that have
become for Christians their companions for seeking a life a prayer. These
include the writings of Ignatius, Francis de Sales, and Teresa of Avila to
name just a few. Their interpersonal exchange of love between themselves

and the Divine, which we call prayer, was rooted in the stuff of their lives. In their book, *Praying for Your Special Needs Child*, David and Mercedes Rizzo have written an inspiring and, I would say, essential companion to prayer for families with a child with disabilities. The book provides a rare and intimate glimpse into the everyday struggles and joys of raising a child with a disability. The stories, the questions to ponder, and the prayers at the end of each chapter assist families to use the real stuff of their lives and the richness of our Catholic prayer tradition to draw closer to God and one another to be sustained and strengthened by the divine presence."

—Sister Kathleen Schipani, IHM, director of the Office for Persons with Disabilities and the Deaf Apostolate, Archdiocese of Philadelphia

"Early in *Praying for Your Special Needs Child*, David and Mercedes Rizzo comment on the struggles they faced in raising their daughter Danielle, who has autism, by writing, 'We needed hope.' With this book, that is exactly what the Rizzos provide to other families in similar situations. They address not only the physical and emotional challenges that came into their lives, but the spiritual ones as well. They had no guidebook on raising a special needs child in the Catholic faith they hold so dear, so they became pioneers who forged a path for themselves that others can now follow. Their journey also led them to a deeper trust in God than they had ever imagined, and helped them discover that answered prayers sometimes look different than we expect. Because of the Rizzos' honesty and hard-won wisdom, *Praying for Your Special Needs Child* will be a blessing to parents who feel overwhelmed by their situation. Chances are it will leave them with the sense of hope they need to move toward a brighter future."

—Tony Rossi, director of communications at The Christophers

PRAYING FOR YOUR

Special Needs Child

David Rizzo and Mercedes McBride Rizzo

theWORD
among us®
press

Published by The Word Among Us Press,
7115 Guilford Drive, Suite 100
Frederick, Maryland 21704
www.wau.org

22 21 20 19 18   1 2 3 4 5

ISBN: 978-1-59325-340-0
eISBN: 978-1-59325-514-5

Cover design by Faceout

Made and printed in the United States of America

Library of Congress Control Number: 2018944083

To our sons, Brendan and Colin,

and to our daughters, Danielle and Shannon.

Acknowledgments

Writing a book requires the help and support of many people. We wish to acknowledge and thank everyone who helped this book come to fruition. First Patty Mitchell at The Word Among Us for reaching out to us with the vision of a book intended to help parents pray for their children with special needs. She knew this book was needed even before we did, and we are honored that she asked us to write it. Additionally, we would like to thank Beth McNamara and Jessica Montgomery for their encouragement and guidance, along with Cindy Cavnar and Lucy Scholand for their important contribution. We thank the team at The Word Among Us who contributed to our book in any way. We wish to thank Phyllis Hartzell for her lifelong friendship and for her photography skills. We thank our parents. Although they are no longer with us we know they are continuing to help us on our journey as parents ourselves. In a special way we thank our children Brendan, Colin, and Shannon for the attention and care they give their sister. It is not easy when your sibling has special needs. And to Danielle, we thank you for being you. Lastly, we thank God for giving us the gift of our children, and allowing us to feel the divine presence in our lives, even during the times that we struggled raising a child with special needs.

CONTENTS

Introduction:
The Gift of Your Special Needs Child

D riving through the New Jersey Pinelands that day, we searched for the shrine. We were desperate for prayer. Our daughter Danielle had been diagnosed with autism. Our family was struggling with what to do. Just a few days before, we had heard of a place many people were flocking to in the hope of obtaining miraculous healing. Since it wasn't that far from where we lived, about an hour away, we put the kids in the car and went to check it out.

We didn't know the area well, and we didn't have an exact street address. We just knew the name of the town and the crossroads. Back then we didn't own a GPS either. So we did what people did in those days. We stopped and asked folks we met, "Do you know how to get to the St. Padre Pio Shrine?" No one seemed to know.

We could have given up, but we were determined to locate the shrine. We wanted to help our daughter. Many people turn to prayer when they feel a sense of desperation. We were no exception. After all, our little girl was diagnosed with a lifelong, life-altering condition, and we wanted her cured.

After a while, we came across a warehouse where some men were loading crates of fruits and vegetables onto a truck. One of the men got all excited when he heard that we were looking for the St. Padre Pio Shrine. He told us he was a frequent visitor there, and he knew exactly which way to go. We scribbled the directions he gave us on a scrap of paper.

A few miles later, the shrine came into view. There it sat on a peaceful, ten-acre corner lot. Many of the faithful had gathered to ask for St. Padre Pio's intercession on their behalf. We could sense the hope in these people, and we needed hope. Certainly we needed prayer.

People were seated on long pews and were praying quietly. Danielle could be loud. Like many kids with autism, she was in constant motion, running from place to place. We hoped she wouldn't run away from us as we walked up to the statue to kneel and pray.

Quite a few years have passed since we visited the St. Padre Pio Shrine. Prayer has been an important part of our life as parents of a child with special needs. Our family has come to rely on prayer but in a very different way than we originally expected.

When we went to the shrine, we were hoping for a complete cure. We wanted God to take away our daughter's autism and give her the gift of speech. We saw prayer as a way to convince God to make the autism go away. We did not know then that prayer works differently. Instead it was to draw us, our whole family, more deeply into Danielle's life as a child with autism and teach us how to live an authentic and joyous life.

Prayer became for us an opportunity to reflect on the challenges Danielle faced. It gave us a way to speak about what Danielle and the rest of us were experiencing, and the concerns we were carrying in our hearts, in a healthy and productive way. Perhaps most importantly, it allowed us to tap into energy that we needed in order to get through each day. It gave us the strength to get up and talk to God.

Prayer sustained us during some very trying times, and it continues to sustain us now. There are days when it flows easily and others when it comes more slowly. It is not just prayer as a petition; it can also take the form of gratitude and celebration. We discovered that listening is a type of prayer too.

We believe fervently that our prayers were heard that day at the shrine. We continued to learn more about prayer from our regular visits there. Padre Pio often said, "Pray, hope, and don't worry." The hardest part is not to worry, but in many ways, that is the secret to successful prayer. We saw people at the shrine leave their burdens and worries at Padre Pio's feet. We found that it's hard not to take the burden back after you leave. We needed to trust that God would answer our prayers in the best way, even if we didn't understand yet what the best way was.

Today we look back on our first visit to the shrine with fondness. Our two boys are now adults. Our two girls are now teenagers in high school. We have learned to trust God with our hopes and dreams for them.

This book will explore how parents can pray for their children with special needs as they face challenges and obstacles, decisions about medical treatments and services, concerns over what the future may bring, and other important issues for families of children with special needs.

At the end of each chapter is a suggested prayer. Chapters 2 through 11 also include three questions to guide you in reflecting on the content as well as a "way to pray" based on our Catholic tradition.

Chapter One

You Are Your Child's Intercessor

Parents have many roles when it comes to raising a child with special needs. One of the most important is interceding for him or her in prayer. Intercession is something parents should do every day. We stand before God and plead from our hearts for help, setting forth our child's needs in as straightforward and clear a way as we can.

Our Catholic tradition gives us examples of parents who interceded on behalf of their children. St. Monica was a faithful intercessor for her son St. Augustine of Hippo. She prayed for his conversion to the faith for seventeen years, never giving up but continuing to raise her mind and heart to God on his behalf. Ultimately Augustine converted and became one of the greatest saints of the Church. Like St. Monica, you can intercede for your child and expect your prayers to be heard.

To stand up and pray takes courage, something you may feel you lack. It may be helpful to recall the courage you have shown when interceding for your child in other ways. It takes courage to advocate for your special needs child in front of doctors, teachers, and insurance companies. Yet you can dig deep and discover the courage to fight those fights on your child's behalf. Take this courage with you when you approach God in prayer.

And you are not alone. Your child has other intercessors. First and foremost, there is Jesus, who intercedes before God the Father on behalf of the entire human race (see Romans 8:34). The saints are powerful intercessors too. Relatives, family, and friends are interceding. You can be confident that others are in the struggles with you.

Praying for Patience

When parents discover their child has a serious disability, they may turn to prayer, as we did, in the hope that God will fix everything in one fell swoop. This is very understandable, because parents are trying to deal with what can seem like complete chaos. Their world has been turned upside down and seems totally unmanageable. This is especially the case when the child is newly diagnosed. Your child might require all your time and attention. You want God to fix the situation and to do it now!

We felt like this when Danielle was around four years old. Not only was she unable to communicate, but she engaged in many challenging behaviors. At one of the healing services we took Danielle to at that time, people were asking the leader of the service to pray over their children. He would pray and say things like "I have a good feeling that God will grant what you are asking for. I know you will get the result that you are seeking."

When it came time for the man to pray for Danielle, we expected to hear that Danielle would be cured of her autism. In fact, we were confident that we would hear this. However, the man said that he felt the need to "pray for patience on the part of Danielle's parents." It took a while for us to understand what he meant by that.

Actually, that was the perfect prayer. It helped us realize that there was to be a long unfolding of God's grace, in which we would gradually discover the powerful presence of God in our lives. And we would discover this precisely because we were parents of Danielle, the beautiful child with autism whom God had given us.

Praying for Peace and Understanding

Kids with disabilities require an enormous amount of parental involvement. You may find yourself assisting your child with tasks and activities, advocating for them in a variety of settings, arranging medical appointments and therapy schedules, and just plain keeping them safe. These things can lead to a very busy household, hectic schedules, high stress levels, and parental burnout.

Parents may long for a sense of peace and serenity. They may doubt themselves and despair about the future. They may doubt God—if he's listening or if he's there at all.

In the midst of all this, it is important to pray for peace and understanding, so you can manage these stresses and feel good about your life. Prayer for peace and understanding will allow you to have the energy you need to properly care for your child and not lose yourself in the process.

You may resent your child for *putting you through this*. You may be angry at friends and family members who aren't going through what you're going through. This is the time to stop and pray. Prayer helps you remember that with God all things are possible (see Luke 1:37) and that he can gift you with a sense of peace and understanding. He can bring you to a place of stillness in the storm.

The key is to trust that you will find meaning in the experience and that you will see God's plan unfold. One day the meaning may hit you in the head like Newton's apple. You will see the positive effect your child has on others and on your family. You will see the child's value as a beloved daughter or son of God. Peace and understanding will flow from this recognition.

In the Book of Proverbs, we are told to trust God with all our hearts. We are told not to lean on our own understanding but on God's (see Proverbs 3:5-8). In the beginning of our walk as parents of a special needs child, our level of understanding was insufficient. God transformed our faulty understanding, but it took time. We had to give up for a time our vision of what we thought life was supposed to be. We had to walk in darkness. Faith and trust gave us night vision and allowed us to make it to dawn.

If we can give any advice to a special needs parent, it is to remember that where you are now is not where you will end up in ten years, five years, or even one year. Progress will be made, and milestones will be met, and you will experience better days. You will have the peace and understanding that you long for.

———————|———————

Dear God, who in your infinite goodness bring all things and all persons into being, to you we now bring ourselves in prayer. You, without whom not even a single sparrow falls, have fashioned our lovely child as a person with special needs and presented them to us as a precious gift. We lift our hearts, minds, and bodies to you on their behalf.

With Jesus, your beloved Son, who on the cross stretched his arms to you on behalf of all men and women, we intercede now for our child. We ask for the powerful intercession of Mary, our Blessed Mother, and of St. Monica, whose daily prayers helped her son become the person you intended him to be. We join with all our friends and family, and all people everywhere who raise their voices on behalf of others, and we ask that your will for our child be done.

We ask you to grant us the patience we need to persist in our role as loving parents and not lose heart or fall into despair. Help us rely on you, on your goodness and divine wisdom. Help us know that all things proceed in their appointed times.

Teach us to understand the right direction. Give us clarity on which path to take. Help us trust in you with all our hearts and not lean on our own limited understanding. Bring us the peace that comes from knowing you and trusting you in all things.

CHAPTER TWO

The Doctor Is In

Part of your parental role is to take your children to the doctor. There will be sick visits and well visits and follow-up visits in between. And when your child has special needs, you will likely spend more time in doctors' offices than you expected or would like. These visits can be hard, especially if your child has difficulty tolerating the waiting room and the doctor's examination.

Prayer comes in handy when you are trying to figure out why your child is in pain. Is it due to something relatively benign or something more serious? Prayer can help you find the right doctors, specialists, and other medical professionals and obtain appointments in a timely manner. Prayer can ease anxiety and fear surrounding medical appointments and diagnoses.

One of the most difficult challenges we have faced in raising our daughter Danielle is her inability to communicate pain and other signs that something is wrong with her medically. Danielle is nonverbal and doesn't know how to let people know what pain she is experiencing. Fortunately, God has been good, and these times have been relatively few. Overall Danielle has been healthy.

However, one day, when Danielle was around nine years old, she began crying for no apparent reason. The crying began intermittently, but after a day it escalated to painful screaming. We knew it was time to take her to the emergency room.

The triage nurse determined that Danielle should be immediately evaluated and moved to the treatment area because of her uncontrolled screaming and obvious pain. We found ourselves silently asking God to ease her discomfort and to allow the ER professionals to quickly and accurately find out what was wrong. It turned out that Danielle had a very painful infection. The doctors gave her an antibiotic, which did the trick. Very soon she returned to her normal happy self.

There have been many other times when Danielle has been tearful—sometimes at two o'clock in the morning and with no obvious cause. We have felt helpless, with that knot in the pit of our stomachs, wondering if we should head once more to the hospital ER. Whenever this happens, we know that it's time to turn our hearts and minds to God, even if it's just for a quick prayer to ground us and put our minds at rest.

Perhaps you have had to take your child to an emergency room and have experienced the same knot in the pit of your stomach that we felt. At such a time, it is often hard to put your feelings into words. When you feel overwhelmed, you may not remember that you can ask God for help. But it's exactly the right time to do so.

Prayer doesn't have to be showy or formal. More often it takes the form of simply quieting down and becoming aware that you are calling out to God. One way to prepare yourself to come into the presence of God is by breathing deeply. After three or four breaths, you can make the Sign of the Cross, remind yourself that God is in control, and relax, knowing that you have put your child in God's hands. You'll feel the tension decrease and your muscles relax.

Asking for divine help puts you in a better state to help your child. If you don't know what words to say, then try this prayer: "Sacred Heart of Jesus, I put my trust in you." Repeat this to yourself. Soon the words will flow naturally, and peace will fill your heart.

Finding the Right Doctors

Children with special needs sure have a lot of doctors. This is especially the case for children with physical disabilities, but kids with developmental disabilities, like autism and Down syndrome, can have accompanying medical problems too.

When dealing with something as important as your child's health, you want medical professionals to be the right people—caring and understanding in their approach, skillful, and knowledgeable about what your child needs. You want to find a doctor whose office is close to your home. You want to get appointments as soon as possible and minimize time spent in the waiting room. Most importantly, you want a medical person who talks to your child compassionately, one who does not dismiss your child because of his or her cognitive and behavioral challenges but rather treats him or her with the dignity that should be given to all people.

Danielle needed glasses when she was in preschool. We needed to find an eye doctor who could evaluate a child who was unable to speak or read an eye chart and whose attention span was very limited. And of course, we wanted one who would treat Danielle with kindness and dignity.

We knew we needed to pray and pray hard. We asked God to bring the right eye doctor into Danielle's life. We asked friends and relatives to pray for us. We included this prayer in our intentions at Mass, and we listed it in the prayer book at our parish. It wasn't long before God brought us a very kind eye doctor, one who diagnosed and treated our daughter's vision problems and, of equal importance, treated her with the dignity she deserves.

Of course, the need for prayer does not end when you find the right doctor. That can be just the beginning of a long list of things to pray for. If you're like us, prayer will become your go-to proactive and reactive strategy to deal with the challenges you face as parents of a special needs child. For instance, we would never have thought something as ordinary as wearing eyeglasses could be a problem. We soon found ourselves asking God to help Danielle overcome the novelty of the glasses, as well as her exaggerated sensory reactions to them.

Each day we would put the glasses on Danielle's face. Both of us would hold her small hands so she could not remove the glasses as we walked around the house and yard. And we would say a prayer that her tolerance for the glasses would improve. Danielle began to accept wearing the glasses for longer and longer intervals. Our prayers really helped us generate the strength and endurance we needed to stick with the plan long enough to see God's handiwork unfold.

When you are dealing with many demands due to your child's medical needs, you can become tired, both physically and emotionally. So how do you use prayer to generate the energy that you need so that you won't give up?

One way is to remember that the first thing God does in the Book of Genesis is to call light into being. God sets the universe in motion by filling it with light. So from the start, God manifests his creative power in a display of energy. If God can bring light into existence, then you can be sure that he has the power to energize you.

Be confident in asking God to provide the energy you need. Think about how the sun showers light upon the earth and fills the world with color and warmth. Now imagine God showering his energy upon you. God's energy is the kind that keeps you in the game. He is the source of all energy. Let this bring you to him when the batteries of your body and soul need to be recharged.

Timely Appointments

A big drain on your energy can be scheduling timely medical appointments. Anyone who has ever scheduled a medical appointment with a specialist knows that you may have to wait several months to be seen. This can become an occasion for prayer. Parents who are already worried about their children and about what the appointment will reveal do not want to wait months!

Before you pick up the phone to schedule an appointment, turn to God to ask for an available date. If it turns out that the appointment can't take place soon, then ask God to reduce your anxiety over the situation.

Before our daughter was diagnosed with autism, we were told there would be a four-month minimum wait to see a neurologist. Four months is a long time in the life of a three-year-old and can seem interminable for parents who want a diagnosis confirmed or ruled out. Prayer helped us deal with the prolonged uncertainty over what was going on with our daughter. Then, out of the blue, we found out about a local neurologist who just happened to have a cancellation that fit our schedule.

When we allow our struggles and challenges to lead us to prayer, we can expect God's help with the things that really matter. Parents of children with special needs are striving to lead an authentic life in the midst of trying times. One of the most trying times is during the diagnostic process, when you are anxious to discover what is going on with your child and make some sense of it. The diagnostic process can be long. There are parental questionnaires that you need to complete, and often the questions can be hard to understand.

This is an excellent time to pray. You can ask God for clarity and for the ability to give an honest assessment about your child, so the doctor has the information needed to make an informed and accurate diagnosis.

When the diagnosis of autism came for our daughter at age four, we had already prayed for the courage to accept her condition. This helped lessen the shock when the diagnosis was finally delivered, though it took longer for us to fully accept her autism as part of God's plan for our family. Once again, prayer helped us trust God and take this step of faith.

A Carrier of Prayer

Many people want to pray and are drawn to prayer when their lives are turned upside down by circumstances and events that are hard to control. People come from different starting places. Some people may have lots of experience with spirituality and prayer. Others may have a very limited experience. Fortunately as human beings, we are all able to access divine mercy and guidance for our souls.

Parents of children with special needs might be walking a long and difficult path. They carry burdens that can weigh them down. Their hearts can become preoccupied with the challenges they and their children encounter. But a great transformation can occur when we choose to see these not as burdens but as guideposts for the soul. They let us know where we are now and where we are going.

We can use these guideposts as something like the plot elements of our life story. Such stories call for a deep response from the soul. In prayer our words percolate upward, and we tell our stories to God. The burdens and anxieties we carry become prayers. They become parts of that great two-way conversation that exists between the soul and God.

When this happens, parents may sense in their own private way that raising a child with special needs is a vocation and that we are now "prayer carriers." This sense can mark a turning point, where we begin to move toward deeper acceptance of our life and, indeed, an embrace of it. We begin to see our children as gifts whom we can cherish.

The Elevator

At this point, we should acknowledge that many families are dealing with very serious medical conditions. There are families who have chronically ill children with complex issues such as seizures. Some children require feeding tubes, restricted diets, and more. When we think about some of these issues, we realize that everyone is walking their own path, and many are suffering more than we can know.

This became apparent to us when we took Danielle to a major children's hospital for a consultation with one of her doctors. After the appointment, we got into the elevator and saw a familiar face. She wasn't anyone we knew all that well but an acquaintance. Although it had been several years since we had seen each other, she recognized us immediately and struck up a conversation. She told us that her own daughter was diagnosed with leukemia, and treatment was not going well.

We didn't know what to say. Nothing seemed to make much sense. All we could really say was that we were sorry. We told her we would pray for her little girl.

We had just come from a very difficult blood draw for Danielle. She had been screaming and crying, completely uncooperative. We were feeling as if we had had enough of this thing called autism. However, the encounter with our friend in the elevator made us really think.

As we came off the elevator, we noticed the hospital chapel. We stopped in and offered a prayer on behalf of the little girl with leukemia. At the same time, we offered a prayer of gratitude that Danielle's blood draw was completed and that she was now smiling and going home with us.

Many years have passed. We never learned what happened to the child with leukemia. But on days when we feel overwhelmed by autism, we can recall with great clarity that chance encounter in the elevator at the children's hospital. It became an opportunity for us to expand our prayers beyond the needs of our own child, to hold up to God the needs of all children with medical concerns and indeed the needs of all people everywhere who suffer, regardless of the cause.

Parents of children with special needs may wish to consciously extend their prayer intentions beyond the needs of their own child. Praying for others helps us develop perspective and compassion. It leads to a deepening of faith and trust, and it can build a sense of solidarity and support among parents who are in similar circumstances.

Tolerating Appointments and Procedures

Attending medical appointments can be a real challenge. Your child may have trouble understanding what is going on and may be in pain or suffering discomfort. He or she may not be able to communicate information. That puts much of the responsibility on parents, who may just be giving their best guess.

The child may not know what is expected and may not know how to behave. Even older kids with special needs may lack sufficient social skills to recognize that there are different rules of behavior in a medical office than at home. Additionally, children may be afraid, especially if they have had negative experiences with doctors or remember uncomfortable procedures, like having a tooth drilled or being held down for a blood draw.

Kids with sensory and developmental challenges may want to wander around the waiting room or grab objects. Waiting areas can be crowded and noisy. Once you get into the examination room area, you may face a whole new set of obstacles. Often these rooms are small and confining.

Children with special needs may have trouble tolerating a physical exam. A routine task like getting blood pressure can cause much anxiety, leading to a child's excessive movement and making it impossible to get an accurate reading. Even stepping on a scale when asked by the doctor or nurse can be difficult.

Given all these potential problems, medical appointments can be long. Going to the doctor can be a source of fear and anxiety for children and their parents. It may be helpful to turn to Scripture for a prayerful understanding of your life.

The Woman with the Hemorrhage

Many of the people who approached Jesus for healing in the Gospels were anxious and afraid. St. Mark tells the story of the woman with the hemorrhage:

Now there was a woman who had been suffering from hemorrhages for twelve years. She had endured much under many physicians, and had spent all that she had; and she was no better, but rather grew worse. She had heard about Jesus, and came up behind him in the crowd and touched his cloak, for she said, "If I but touch his clothes, I will be made well." Immediately her hemorrhage stopped; and she felt in her body that she was healed of her disease. Immediately aware that power had gone forth from him, Jesus turned about in the crowd and said, "Who touched my clothes?" And his disciples said to him, "You see the crowd pressing in on you; how can you say, 'Who touched me?'" He looked all around to see who had done it. But the woman, knowing what had happened to her, came in fear and trembling, fell down before him, and told him the whole truth. He said to her, "Daughter, your faith has

made you well; go in peace, and be healed of your disease."
(Mark 5:25-34)

We can imagine how the woman with the hemorrhage felt.
We are told that she was afraid and even trembling. Yet Jesus
responded by praising her for her strong faith and healing her
of her affliction.

Jesus is the archetypical healer. We can reach out to him in
prayer by imagining our children with special needs touching
the hem of his garment. We can close our eyes and imagine what
it feels like to receive his healing power. We can visualize Jesus
telling our children, "Your faith has made you well; go in peace,
and be healed of your disease."

Let's carry this image with us when we bring our children to
doctors and other medical professionals. We can be confident
that these meetings will yield fruit. For us, one example of this
fruit is Danielle's progress at dental appointments.

Look, Mom, No Cavities!

Dental appointments are challenging for everyone. No one is
overjoyed to have their teeth drilled or their mouth probed. Even
a routine dental cleaning can be uncomfortable. When you add
a child with special needs to this mix, things can get even more
intense. Some children must be put under general anesthesia just
to have their teeth cleaned.

Dental checkups for Danielle proved to have lots of ups and
downs. In the beginning, the dentist, the hygienist, and both of us
had to hold her securely in the chair: the dentist and hygienist at

her head, David holding her legs, Mercedes holding her arms and reassuring Danielle that they were almost done and that this was going to help her. David would have to take time off from work to help with the appointments. We dreaded these dental appointments with Danielle. Our prayer was always for no cavities.

Finding a dentist who specializes in treating children with special needs was very helpful. The dental staff was patient and kind to Danielle, explaining things in a soft voice and with a gentle manner. They developed a routine with her, doing the same steps in the same order. We would prep Danielle in advance about what was going to happen.

It took years, but today Danielle sits in the dental chair all by herself. She is cooperative with the dentist and hygienist. Just recently her dentist remarked on how far we have come. Our prayers have been answered.

Imagine that you are standing outside your child's dentist office. You are feeling anxious about walking in. The last time you brought your child here, it did not go well. As you place your hand on the doorknob, pause and ask God to help you.

What will you ask for? Ask yourself what you need God to do here. It is okay to ask God for an easy appointment. It is okay to ask God for no cavities. Relax, and visualize yourself walking through the door knowing that God is in control of this appointment.

Questions

1. What is your greatest concern about your child's medical health? Have you asked God for help? How did you do this?
2. How do you feel when you take your child to the doctor or for tests? What do you want to say to God at these times?
3. What prayer are you carrying in the deepest corner of your heart? Is this best expressed in words or in silence?

A Prayer of Petition
Is One Way to Pray

Many of the prayer suggestions given in this chapter involve asking God to help us with specific challenges that children with special needs and their parents face. God knows what we want and need, even if we don't. Putting those wants and needs into words helps us understand what is on our minds and in our hearts and what is troubling us. Praying this way clarifies things for us, but more importantly, it allows us to let go of our powerlessness and give our problems to God.

When we do this, we no longer have to worry about the ultimate outcome. We have left that to God. Relieved of that burden, we can live in the present moment, aligned with the will of God. We can love and nurture our families, ourselves, and others.

Dear God, we come to you with our burdens. Help us know that you are writing our family's story and that the twists and turns of our life will lead us to you. May we become transparent and reveal to you the longings of our soul. May our fears and anxieties be replaced by the calm silence that flows out of our communion with you.

Seeking healing on behalf of our child's health and medical concerns, we reach out to you as did the woman with the hemorrhage. We ask that our child with special needs experience the same power in their life.

We ask that you bring the right doctors and other medical professionals into our child's life. May they look at our child with deeply compassionate eyes and see not just a child with special needs but also a child of God. May they possess the technical and medical skills that our child needs. May they handle fears and concerns with kindness and gentleness. We ask that they have the patience to explain procedures and perform thorough evaluations. May all who work with our child show persistence and build appropriate and helpful routines, so that our child will grow in the ability to understand and tolerate medical appointments, tests, and procedures.

Lastly, we hold up to you, O God, all children with special needs and medical concerns, their parents and families, that they may feel your love and healing presence. May they know happiness and peace. May all people everywhere be healed in body and soul and know that they are children of God!

Chapter Three

Praying for Your Child's Education

We were not rookie parents when Danielle came along. She is our third child. We were "experienced," if that even means anything when you are talking about parenthood. We knew the basics: the two a.m. feedings, the teething, and the wonderful world of colic.

Our first son, Brendan, days before his second birthday, formed words and sentences about his new brother, Colin. Two years later, Colin was speaking in complete sentences. We fully expected Danielle to follow suit. Her babbling, we thought, would turn into words and then into full sentences by two or three years of age.

But things were different. We heard a few words from Danielle, like *Mama, Dada*, and *kitty cat,* but they were hard to understand. The stringing of words into sentences never emerged, and after a while, she even stopped saying the few words she had managed to learn.

At a well-baby checkup, the pediatrician told us that we should take Danielle to an early intervention program, which would evaluate her and provide services if developmental delays or disabilities so indicated. Early intervention was the beginning of Danielle's formal education. She was only two years old.

Education plays a very important part in the lives of children with special needs. Parents can make a lot of difference by advocating for specialized services and accommodations.

This can be draining. It often brings out the fight in parents who want the best for their special needs child. The challenge can give rise to a wide range of emotions, some good and some not so good.

We found ourselves turning to prayer—not only to help Danielle overcome the educational challenges she faced but also to help us deal with what we were feeling: the sadness, the anger, the helplessness, and the isolation. We also prayed for the wisdom to make smart choices on Danielle's behalf.

When an eligible child is three years of age, the responsibility for education shifts from the early intervention program to the local school district. We thought that early intervention would address and correct what we saw as a temporary speech delay. We never thought that Danielle had a serious neurological disability like autism. We had no idea that we would be in it for the long run.

Every now and then, the speech therapist or occupational therapist working with Danielle would try to point us to the thought that maybe this was more than just a temporary speech delay. When Danielle's occupational therapist mentioned the possibility of autism, we were unprepared. David became very angry and asked that the OT be removed from the case.

Early intervention can be difficult for special needs parents. It's there that you come face-to-face for the first time with many of your child's unique challenges. It's a good time to pray for strength in accepting whatever the future might bring for your child. Pray too for the ability to pay attention to what therapists and other educational professionals have to say, without letting anger or other negative emotions get in the way.

Praying to Move Beyond the Anger

So much changes when you become the parent of a child with special needs. It's easy to get caught up in a whirlwind of disappointment and lose control of your emotions. The dreams and expectations you had for your child start to fall apart, and without even knowing why, you find yourself feeling angry. Look, nobody is perfect, and given all that's happening, it's perfectly normal to feel anger and other negative emotions. It's an important and valid part of processing what's going on in your life.

However, there comes a time when you realize that the anger is intensifying and prolonging your pain, that it is getting in the way of progress and blocking you from the healing that you and your family need. When this time comes, it's helpful to reach out to God in prayer. Ask him to move you beyond the anger, isolation, sorrow, and other painful emotions you're feeling.

One way to do this is to reflect on the loving nature of God and his desire for us to be happy. Begin by sitting in a relaxed position. Close your eyes, and make the Sign of the Cross. Breathe in and out deeply, and repeat silently, "God created me to share in his happiness and peace." Allow the prayer to flow smoothly to the measure of each inhale and exhale. "God created me to share in his happiness and peace."

Continue to do this for as long as you feel comfortable. Just allow the words to sound in your mind and heart, as you become more deeply aware that God truly wants your anger to be transformed into genuine happiness. This prayer is reminiscent of the Jesus Prayer, which was popular among monks and nuns who devoted themselves to prayer in the desert in the first few centuries of the Christian era. In a similar way, we can prepare our souls to receive the happiness and peace that God offers us.

The Preschool Disabled Program

You may have trouble coming to grips with sending your three-year-old child with special needs off to the local school district's preschool disabled program. You may be fearful. Your child may still be in diapers or lack the ability to talk or walk. He or she may have very complicated medical concerns.

You are being told, by people you don't know and haven't had time to develop trust in, that you need to send your child to a school with a teacher and aides. You may wonder if the teacher and aides will be kind to your child. Will they be able to handle the behavioral and medical needs of your child?

Attending school is a big change for both you and your child. You may feel overwhelmed by all the new challenges. You can meet these challenges with prayers for a successful transition to school.

You can ask God to provide teachers and aides who are kind and understanding, who don't lose their tempers, and who recognize how to deal with the physical, cognitive, and behavioral issues that affect your child. You can pray that you have sufficient trust in these teachers and caretakers. You can pray that your child develop strong communication, motor, and social skills.

You might pray that your child make progress in toileting and hygiene. A preschool disabled program is frequently where children with intellectual and developmental disabilities graduate from diapers to underpants. You can pray that the school help your special needs child master this important task.

On the Road Again

Transportation issues associated with school can present significant challenges to children with special needs. These include handicapped accessibility, the length of time spent on the bus, accommodations such as air conditioning and support staff, and overall safety.

Parents may be worried about the length of the bus ride, about safety and comfort, and about their child being scared. These were our concerns, especially since Danielle is nonverbal and could not make her needs known or tell us how the day went. This was all new territory for us. We were unfamiliar with how to advocate for her.

When we learned that Danielle would be on the bus for a long time and that the bus route would be complex, we decided to forgo the bus and drive her to school ourselves. Eventually Danielle rode the school bus, but it took a while for us to be truly comfortable with it. Parents might want to pray that their child's educational needs can be met in a school close to home.

You can pray that appropriate transportation personnel—such as a bus aide or nurse—be provided. Ask God for staff who are trained in your child's unique needs and prepared to act in any medical emergency. If necessary, pray that sufficient space be available for equipment such as oxygen, wheelchairs, crutches, and other assistive devices.

Safety is a tremendous concern for parents. Pray for door-to-door pickup and drop-off, especially if your school district is not in agreement that this is important. Pray that the district understand that your child needs supervision while waiting for the bus and may have difficulty waiting. Pray that the school district understand that children with special needs and their parents often have difficulty sleeping and hence have challenging mornings, that they may need a few extra minutes to be ready for the bus. Pray that the district appreciate the problems bad weather presents, especially for children who use wheelchairs. Lastly, pray that the bus driver remember to wait for the child to get into the house safely and ensure that someone is there to greet them.

Stay in Sync

Wouldn't it be nice if you could stay linked by prayer with your special needs child throughout the school day? This would allow you to remember that God is with your child, keeping watch and helping them make the most of the school experience.

One way to do this is to familiarize yourself with your child's school schedule. Then, at key points of the day, offer a prayer of gratitude to God for guiding your child. Ask him to ease their fears, reduce anxiety, and promote successful learning and overall well-being.

Think about this as a sort of Liturgy of the Hours, by which you mark specific times of the day with a prayer. For example, if your child is riding the bus at 8:15, turn your mind toward God at this time, and imagine how he is preparing a safe and happy bus experience for your child. When circle time starts at 9:00, thank God for your child's developing social skills and ability to learn classroom rules and routines. At 10:00, when the adaptive physical education teacher leads the class in a gross-motor activity, you might offer up a prayer that your child progress in physical skill, have fun, and make friends. Making your intentions specific to your child's schedule will help you pray for them throughout the day.

IEP: Three Letters Parents Know and Dread

If your child receives special education services, they will undoubtedly have a document called an Individualized Education Plan (IEP). This document is developed each year by the school district's child-study team and the child's parents, in accordance with federal and state special education law. The IEP sets forth the services the school district must provide to support the education of children who meet special education eligibility standards. It is an individualized plan. This means it is designed specifically for each child, to meet that child's unique needs.

So why do we say that this document is *dreaded*? We say this because you will advocate for your child year after year. Remember, the team of professionals sitting across the table from you may have ideas about what is necessary, feasible, or cost-worthy that do not align with your expectations. The conflict can be combative and draining. There's a good chance that afterward you may feel as if you're returning from battle.

An example of the challenges the IEP presents is obtaining what is known as *related services*. These include physical, occupational, and speech therapies, among others. Many kids with disabilities benefit greatly from these services. However, there can be considerable disagreement between you and the school district on which therapies are needed, whether they are given in individual or group sessions, how many days a week, and the goals and objectives of each.

We have advocated for Danielle in these meetings. On more than one occasion, we had to put on our boxing gloves and step into the ring. Our school district was not always sold on our ideas, and it could take a bit of negotiation to come to a mutually acceptable agreement. We were really worn down in many of these IEP sessions.

Over the years, we learned to spend at least thirty minutes sitting quietly in prayer and meditation before walking into an IEP meeting. Prayer can be very calming, putting you in a more fit spiritual condition so that you do not lose your temper or make rash judgements. Prayer helps you size up what people are saying and respond accordingly.

Danielle has made a lot of progress in her related services. Truly this is an answer to prayers that the right therapists would be found and that we would have the knowledge and vision to ask for the right services, as well as the courage to not back down.

Praying for Strength

Many parents of children with special needs fight just as hard, pray just as hard, and are just as exhausted with the IEP process as we have been. Parents need to cultivate strength, or they may be tempted to throw in the towel and give up. They need more than mere strength of body. They need deep spiritual strength. This kind of strength comes from prayer.

But what does it mean to pray for spiritual strength? How do you go about it?

Praying for spiritual strength means asking to be moved by the same energy that moves all of creation, from the tiniest atoms to the largest stars and galaxies. It is no less than asking for the breath of God to fill your lungs as you breathe and to be carried by your blood into the very tissues of your body. It is prayer that your limited and frail self step aside so that God can work in you and manifest himself in you without your weakness getting in the way.

When we pray for spiritual strength, we are asking that our spirit be aligned with the Holy Spirit. We are asking to have the faith of a mustard seed, which by allowing God to dictate its actions, grows into a sturdy tree, expansive enough for birds to nest in (see Matthew 13:31-32). That is true strength!

One way to pray for spiritual strength is to meditate on those who have shown it. We can look to Mary, the Mother of God. When the angel Gabriel approached the young woman from Nazareth, he told her not to be afraid but to trust the plans God had for her. Mary's natural inclination might have been to be afraid. After all, she was young. She was unsure of what lay ahead. Perhaps she worried what Joseph or her family might think. But bravely she answered yes, and with this she allowed herself to become the mother of Our Lord. She asked for her life to unfold in accordance with the will of God, that the same energy that held together the heavens and the earth would become incarnate in her.

We can look at our children with special needs and consider how much strength they show in their lives. Just thinking about how hard these kids work and how much progress they make can be inspiring. We can pray for spiritual strength by reflecting on that and by honoring their hard work and their determination to succeed.

Questions

1. What do you worry about most when it comes to your child's education? Talk to God from the heart about this, and ask him for help.
2. When preparing for your IEP meetings, ask God to give you the skills you need to be an effective advocate for your child.
3. Identify at least one area relative to your child's education where you need to step aside and trust God to take control. How might you answer yes to God's plan?

A Breath Prayer
Is One Way to Pray

The prayer we introduced to overcome anger is an example of a breath prayer. This type of prayer has been practiced by Christians since at least the third century. You inhale as you speak a phrase and exhale as you finish the statement. Often you pronounce the phrase interiorly—that is, thinking it rather than saying it as you breathe in and out.

The Jesus Prayer is the most famous example of a breath prayer. To pray the Jesus Prayer, you inhale and, in your mind, pronounce, "Lord Jesus Christ," and then breathe out as you similarly pronounce, "have mercy on me." This type of prayer concentrates the mind and leads to deep peace.

You can use breath prayer for a variety of needs, adapting the words as appropriate.

———————————|———————————

Dear God, you have fashioned each one of us with your loving hands. You have given us knowledge and learning to develop the skills and tools we need to walk the path you have laid for us. You have given us teachers to shape us for the journey.

We ask that you help us see the importance of education for children with special needs, especially when our children are very young. Please give us the strength we need to entrust our special children to teachers and to know that this is a sign of our love for them, a recognition that we want the best for them even when circumstances are hard for us. Replace the fear and anxiety in our hearts with peace and joy at seeing each new skill and accomplishment. Help us let go of whatever guilt or trepidation we may feel.

Bring us teachers, aides, therapists, and others who are caring and compassionate and able to develop our child's skills and bring their knowledge to new heights. Help these educators support us by keeping us informed of the many successes that are taking place in our child's life each day in school. Help us work with them to advance our child in all areas.

Help us develop a strong and effective working part-nership with the school district's child-study team. Bring us into agreement on placement, curriculum, and the cor-rect array of services. Lead us to the best approaches, strategies, and technologies. May the right resources fall into place for the benefit of our child.

Give us strength and endurance to advocate for our child. Help us to not give up, even when things don't seem to be going well. Help us to be firm and strong, to remain civil and not burn any bridges.

In this way, Lord, may our child learn and grow into the person they are meant to become. May they attain their highest potential. May we all grow and develop together as we draw near to you.

CHAPTER FOUR

Praying for Your Child's Safety

Children with special needs face challenges to their safety every single day. This is true for children with developmental and cognitive disabilities as well as those with physical disabilities. Parents of children with special needs are acutely aware of these challenges. They find safety one of their biggest sources of concern and anxiety.

Everyday activities and situations—such as a trip to the grocery store, an unattended front door, and crossing the street—can be dangerous. Things you wouldn't think of as unsafe can pose safety problems. Children might put items like shampoo, hand sanitizer, laundry detergent, crayons, and glue in their mouths. These can be toxic or at least cause serious stomach upset.

When Danielle was young, we discovered that, because of her autism, she had a condition known as PICA, a tendency to put nonedible items in her mouth. Danielle's list included liquid soap, shampoo, and hand sanitizer. She would swirl such liquids around in her mouth before spitting them out.

We vigilantly tried to keep such items away from Danielle, but how do you eliminate items like soap? We needed access to such items, as did our other kids and guests in our home. We tried many strategies, from hiding the items to taping the lids shut so Danielle couldn't open them. But she was skillful and opportunistic. She could get to the soap or shampoo in the blink of an eye. The next thing we knew, we were on the phone with poison control. When we took Danielle to the supermarket, she might run over to a janitor's bucket and try to put cleaning supplies in her mouth.

The PICA behavior lasted for several years. Fortunately, the behavior vanished as mysteriously as it had arrived. Nowadays Danielle shows little interest in putting nonedible items in her mouth. The dangerous behavior that caused us so much fear and anxiety, and for which we prayed earnestly for a solution, is gone.

If your child does some dangerous things, you know how draining and nerve-wracking it can be. If you are exhausted by trying to keep your child safe, it is time to surrender the situation to God. This means doing the best you can to maintain the safety of your child and asking God to handle the rest. A prayer of surrender is an act of faith and trust in God, a willingness to accept reality however it unfolds. You surrender your personal desires in favor of God's desires.

This is a difficult prayer to pray. We are not used to surrender; it seems too much like defeat. However, when we realize that we are actually surrendering the burden of having to know everything in advance and make all the right moves and never make a mistake, then surrender becomes a handing over to God, who is our champion in the field. This type of surrender liberates us.

So when you are at your wit's end, hand the burden over to God in a prayer of surrender. Speak to God from your heart, and tell him that you are worried about your child's safety. Tell him you are handing all your concerns to him.

Strolling Along

Pedestrian safety is a real concern for all children but especially for those with special needs. The stakes are high. There is always a chance that a child could venture into the street and be hit by a car.

Of course, we try to teach safe pedestrian behavior to our children. However, in Danielle's case, it took a really long time for it to sink in. Her impulsivity was high. She seemed to have no safety awareness, and she was really fast. Many parents of children with special needs have similar concerns.

Parents can pray for their kids with special needs to better understand the basics of what stop signs and crosswalks mean. They can ask God for success when teaching that curbs represent boundaries that shouldn't be crossed without permission from parents. Pray that your child realize that streets and roads are for cars and off limits otherwise. Pray that your child understand how important it is to watch out for children on swings at the playground and not walk right in front of them.

Prayers like these can help you and your child stay focused on what matters when it comes to safety. They can form an agenda for you and others to follow when teaching pedestrian safety skills to special needs children.

A huge fear of parents of children with special needs is that the kids will get out of the house on their own. We have heard numerous stories from parents about children finding creative ways to do this without the parents' being aware. We once heard someone refer to their child as "Little Houdini." This mother said that it did not matter how many locks she put on the door, her son would figure out a way to escape.

We experienced this type of fear with Danielle. We went to our church carnival, and somehow in the crowd, we got separated from her. We were frantic. We could imagine Mary and Joseph feeling like this when Jesus was lost in the Temple. After quite a long time—but not three days—we found Danielle sitting on a chair in the food court as if nothing was wrong.

When you are concerned about your child's safety, take a few minutes to pray to Mary, the mother of Jesus. In your prayer, recall how frightened she must have felt when Jesus was lost and they were searching everywhere for him. Ask Mary and Joseph to intercede and keep your child safe. Know that they understand what you are feeling, and trust in them to bring this concern before Jesus.

Praying the Psalms

A great way for parents of children with special needs to pray for their child's safety and reduce their own stress is to pray the psalms. We know firsthand that special needs parents are limited in the amount of time they can give to any particular activity, including prayer. That is why we selected the psalms. Each psalm is a fairly short poem or song, and many of them appeal to God for safety and security during truly difficult times. Praying the psalms is a perfect way to engage one's fear by drawing strength and wisdom from the word of God. In the Book of Psalms, we can enter into a kinship with the psalmist, who also turned to God for divine help.

Let's look at one of our favorite examples:

You who live in the shelter of the Most High,
    who abide in the shadow of the Almighty,
will say to the LORD, "My refuge and my fortress;
    my God, in whom I trust."
For he will deliver you from the snare of the fowler
    and from the deadly pestilence;
he will cover you with his pinions,
    and under his wings you will find refuge;
    his faithfulness is a shield and buckler.
You will not fear the terror of the night,
    or the arrow that flies by day,
or the pestilence that stalks in darkness,
    or the destruction that wastes at noonday. (Psalm 91:1-6)

Slowly read through the lines out loud, as you place full trust in God's power to deliver your child from danger. Some of the images may seem strange in our day and age, but put yourself into the psalm as if you and your child with special needs were facing these threats together. One of the most comforting images is that of God as a protective bird covering you with his pinions, meaning his feathers. Know that nothing can harm your child or you when you seek refuge under his wings.

My Guardian Dear

Children with complex medical issues—seizures, decreased mobility, feeding tubes, breathing problems, and other concerns—need continual prayer for their overall health, safety, and comfort.

They may be at risk for injury from falls, pressure wounds, aspiration, and pneumonia.

In our Catholic tradition, we often speak about guardian angels, one of whom accompanies each of us and helps keep us safe and secure. Parents of children with special medical needs can envision their child's guardian angel at work, protecting and keeping him or her out of harm's way. Visualization can be a powerful form of prayer that brings a sense of peace.

You might try it: Choose a good time, when you won't be disturbed. This could be when your child is at school, has gone to bed for the night, or has not yet wakened in the morning. Close your eyes as you sit in a quiet place. Picture in your mind's eye your child going through the day with the guardian angel beside him or her.

If your child is prone to seizures, imagine the angel providing a soft landing should your child start to seize. If your child has a feeding tube, picture the guardian angel holding the child's body at the correct angle, to prevent problems with aspiration. If your child uses platform crutches, envision the angel guiding the crutch tips to smooth surfaces and around obstacles. If your child is on supplemental oxygen, picture the angel monitoring the tank, to ensure that there is a sufficient amount and that all proper safety procedures are being followed.

You can adapt this type of prayer for any medical concern your child faces. At the conclusion of your prayer, remember to thank your child's guardian angel for their diligence and protection.

Questions

1. Has your child ever become separated from you or lost? How did it make you feel? Whom did you turn to for help?
2. What would you ask of Mary to help keep your child safe? How do you think she would respond?
3. In what ways has your guardian angel protected you from harm? In what ways have your children's guardian angels protected them?

Visualization
Is One Way to Pray

In this chapter, we introduced a type of prayer in which we use our imagination to visualize our child's guardian angel providing safety. Visualization, sometimes called imaginative prayer, has deep roots in our Christian tradition, most notably because of St. Ignatius of Loyola's Spiritual Exercises. We can picture a scene in detail, perhaps one from the Gospels, and put ourselves in it. This is a wonderful opportunity to interact with God in a nonverbal, picturesque way.

Since we mentioned the Gospel story of Mary and Joseph finding Jesus in the Temple, try an imaginative prayer based on this. Quiet your mind, placing your awareness on the inhales and exhales of your breathing. Then picture yourself and your child in the scene, and let your prayer develop from there.

Remember, this type of prayer is more about visualization and less about thinking in words or language. Allow yourself to be open to the presence of God and what he is doing in your heart.

———————————|———————————

Dear God, all-powerful and ever-loving God, to whom we turn with our fears and worries, gather us toward you, and take from us the burdens of our hearts. You protect us and shield us from the dangers we face. You cover us with your protective wings, and we draw strength and stand firm in your embrace. We come to you to pray for the safety and security of our child with special needs.

May our child learn how to distinguish things that are safe from things that are dangerous. May they develop the best possible judgement. Help us teach them to respect stop signs, crosswalks, and motor vehicles. May our child never stray so far that they are unable to find their way home. Send your angels, Lord, to protect our child from all physical and psychological harm.

God, our creator and protector, help us weather the storms that threaten us. May we learn from adversity and struggle, and may we put our trust in you, now and forever.

CHAPTER FIVE

The Balancing Act

Parents of a child with special needs may find themselves caught in a balancing act. There are a lot of plates in the air at any given time. It's not easy to attend to the needs of your child with the disability, your other kids, your spouse, your career, and yourself. We have to figure out how to keep all the plates spinning and not crashing down.

In addition to Danielle, we have three other children: Brendan, Colin, and Shannon. There were many times when it felt as if, out of necessity, we were giving Danielle most of our attention, and the other three were missing out. Giving fair and balanced attention to all our children was a great concern.

When our kids were growing up, there were many events going on, as well as our own time-consuming work obligations. Therapy and medical appointments for Danielle competed with these. Often we lacked the energy to focus on everything. Trying to balance it all threatened our family's sense of peace and serenity. We knew we were not alone in this. The challenge has been big for many special needs families we have known.

When Danielle was newly diagnosed with autism, one of the therapies that she received was Applied Behavior Analysis (ABA). She was to receive this therapy every day after school. This meant having a steady stream of therapists on our doorstep, sometimes even before Danielle's bus arrived home. There was little privacy in our home while dinner was being prepared and homework was being done. It seemed as if everyone in the family had to be on their best behavior at all times. We could not let our hair down and relax after a long day at school or work. It was hard to get to other activities on time, and this brought stress, frustration, and hurt feelings.

Prayer offered us a way to deal with these feelings and difficulties. It allowed us to step out of the chaos and focus on something other than the endless parade of therapists. It allowed us to do more than just react to the disruptions all about us but instead to maintain a peaceful demeanor. We learned how to balance things in our family life.

We found new opportunities to pray. Sometimes this meant simply breathing more deeply as we tried to give our full attention to what one or another of the kids was doing, to be present and engaged in their interests and activities. Prayer doesn't have to be formal or even involve words. It doesn't have to involve petitions. Going about one's daily affairs while allowing life to unfold for good or bad, not trying to run away from what God is doing, can be a very powerful prayer. It can bring balance and serenity to you and your family.

How do you pray like this when so much of your time is spent putting out the fires caused by your child's disability?

Try this: Next time you feel exhausted and overwhelmed, and one of your kids comes to you and says he wants you to see or do something that involves him, resist the urge to react immediately. After all, your first reaction will probably be to explain why you can't do it at the moment. Instead, stay silent and breathe deeply in and out three times. With the first breath, think to yourself, "God is working in my family's life." With the second breath, think, "This child is delivering a message from

God." And with the third breath, "God gives me strength to respond serenely and attend to his messages."

At this point, answer your child. Often you will find yourself doing so in a more caring and loving way than your first impulse would have allowed.

Look for ways to reconnect prayerfully with your children. You can alternate having one parent stay home with your special needs child while the other parent takes the other kids to visit an historic or architecturally significant church in your area. Walk through the church, take in the stained-glass windows, smell the incense. Be creative, and have a peaceful and prayerful time together.

Another option is to participate with your children in an event sponsored by their school or religious education program.

Marriage and Self-Interest

Have you put aside your own interests and enjoyments due to the constant demands of special needs parenting? Does this leave you feeling exhausted, overwhelmed, sad, and resentful? Do you feel more like special needs caretakers than like a couple?

We found it hard to keep our balance as a couple. If we had one chance for a do-over, we would find more opportunities for a reprieve from autism. We would leave Danielle with a competent babysitter and go out together. It took us a while to learn how to do this.

For starters, try ninety minutes of prayerful time together. Perhaps an older child, a neighbor, or one of your parents can stay with your special needs child while you attend Mass or a parish retreat.

Even when you don't have a babysitter, you can find quality time to spend together. Through the years, we became creative at this. For instance, we would go out to lunch after Danielle's IEP meetings. We learned that it was important to use these times to discuss matters other than our child's disability, to focus instead on what was going on with us individually and as a couple.

It's essential to find time for things each of you likes to do. Often parenting pushes your activities, your pursuits, and your hobbies out of the way. You may even have forgotten what these are. Prayer can help you reconnect with yourself. Feeding your spirit with silence and inner reflection in a prayerful environment can reestablish the order and sanity you need and help you rediscover yourself.

We suggest you look for opportunities for refreshment in your day, even little pockets of time nestled between the big activities. Perhaps you can take a few minutes during your lunch break to pause and say a quick Hail Mary or Our Father. You might even have time to stop in a nearby church, chapel, or other quiet place of reflection. Light a candle, sit in silence, and pray, maybe just following the rhythms of your breathing. You will return to work feeling refreshed and renewed.

At times you and your spouse may need to trade off parenting responsibilities, so that one of you is free for some refreshment. Remember to reverse the roles next time, so both of you have opportunities to explore reflective and rejuvenating activities.

Beating the Bus Home

Finding appropriate childcare for our daughter produces a large amount of stress, which fuels our need for prayer. You may be experiencing this challenge. Perhaps you are trying to balance your career and the need for sufficient income with caring for your child.

Early in our marriage, we thought we had it all planned out. Mercedes would stay at home while our kids were young, and when they were all in school, she would go back to work. That didn't happen as planned. Even now, every afternoon when Danielle comes home from school, someone in our family needs to be there to get her off the bus, watch her, and keep her safe. You can imagine the juggling act this has been.

You may experience a similar juggling act. You need a job that coincides with your child's school schedule. You find yourself trying to balance career with childcare and making lots of sacrifices in the process. No matter how old your child is, you need to be prepared for inclement weather days, early dismissals, delayed openings, teacher in-services, school holidays, and summer vacation.

We seek help from God about these issues on a daily basis. Sometimes we find ourselves rushing to beat the bus home, with a prayer on our lips and in our hearts. It goes something like this: "Lord, please don't let there be a bridge closure. Please don't let us catch all the red lights. Please don't let a tire go flat. We need to beat the bus home."

To Everything There Is a Season

When we look at the world around us, we see that that there are rhythms and cycles to virtually everything. This is as true at the level of our individual human existence as it is at that of vast galaxies. Learning to live in a way that honors these rhythms and cycles helps us move through life with a renewed sense of dignity and calm.

Knowing that life ebbs and flows in the ways that God intends is part of what faith is all about. This recognition helps to ground us. It ensures that we keep the proper plates in the air and eliminate those that interfere or run counter to a successful balancing act.

Honoring the sacred as it unfolds in the rhythms, cycles, and seasons of our lives does not mean that everything that happens to us is fair or just. Certainly it does not mean that we sugarcoat the negative aspects of our lives, as if the pain and suffering we face isn't really there. Instead it is a bold statement on our part that we trust the changing seasons and the God who sits above them, silent and still. When we connect to God and discover this silence and stillness, we find the energy and strength we need to meet the competing and even conflicting demands of life.

One way to cultivate such trust is to prayerfully read the following passage from the Book of Ecclesiastes:

> For everything there is a season, and a time for every matter
>   under heaven:
> a time to be born, and a time to die;
> a time to plant, and a time to pluck up what is planted;

a time to kill, and a time to heal;

a time to break down, and a time to build up;

a time to weep, and a time to laugh;

a time to mourn, and a time to dance;

a time to throw away stones, and a time to gather
    stones together;

a time to embrace, and a time to refrain from embracing;

a time to seek, and a time to lose;

a time to keep, and a time to throw away;

a time to tear, and a time to sew;

a time to keep silence, and a time to speak;

a time to love, and a time to hate;

a time for war, and a time for peace. (Ecclesiastes 3:1-8)

We see in this passage that life runs the gamut from birth to death. There are ups and downs, happiness and joy, violence and healing—times for each. We do best when we structure our lives in accordance with the patterns and flows in which we find ourselves and recognize the sacred there.

God calls us to a life of change and stillness at the same time. He asks us to embrace the seasons as they arise, exist, and fall away. We must learn how to trust God and balance the plates that are spinning around us and high above us.

Questions

1. What are you trying to balance in your life? In what ways has this balance been more difficult because of having a child with special needs?

2. Have you ever needed to abandon your shopping cart at the supermarket or leave an appointment early to rush home to meet your child arriving from school? How did this make you feel? What steps did you take or could you take to avoid this situation?

3. How do you honor the rhythms and seasons of your life? In what ways does this renew your spirit and fill you with hope?

Reading Scripture
Is One Way to Pray

Scripture can be a great entry point to prayer. The Church venerates our sacred texts as the inspired word of God. They form the bedrock of our faith and are highly beneficial for study and prayer.

We read Scripture prayerfully when we allow the words and images to work in us and connect us to the same divine energy that inspired the authors. When read this way, Scripture leads us into our own intimate relationship with God, who nourishes us and makes us whole. The passage from the Book of Ecclesiastes in this chapter is part of the wisdom books in the Hebrew Scriptures, which also include Job, Psalms, Proverbs, Wisdom, Song of Songs, and Sirach. These books form a rich wellspring from which to pray.

Once again, dear God, we carry ourselves to you, to lie down beside your deep, life-affirming waters. Help us draw the strength and energy we need to fully engage life and embrace the present moment with serenity and joy. Most of all, help us find the balance we need to respond attentively to all our children, so that each may know how much we love them.

Keep us free from partiality. May we water all the flowers entrusted to us, and may they bloom and open their petals to you, O Lord!

Help us also find time to devote to our marriage. You brought us together to celebrate your great love. May we never become so focused on the task of parenting that we fail to spend time together as a couple. May you remind us of the value of candlelit dinners and romantic movies, shared cups of coffee and loving conversation.

Likewise, Lord, help us reconnect with our individual selves, our own interests and aspirations. Remind us of the words you've whispered in our silent hours, and help us honor them. Let us take seriously your calls and proddings. Let us respect how you fashion the desires of our souls. We trust that a balanced pursuit of our dreams will strengthen us and that this strength will spill over into all parts of our lives.

Help us with practical matters too. Help us balance our parenting responsibilities with the need for gainful and productive employment. Allow us to cover the gaps in our schedules, so that when we are at work, we can devote our full selves to the tasks at hand. Help us cover unexpected snow days and early dismissals, school hol-idays and teachers' in-services.

Help us find trustworthy babysitters and childcare workers, so that we will not feel torn between the very important responsibilities of caring for our children and the other needs and desires of our lives and our relation-ships. Help us honor the rhythms and cycles of our lives, that we might discover the sacred in our midst. Help us keep the plates spinning.

Chapter Six

Money, Money

Parents have plenty of things to buy. Starting out, you need to pay for diapers, a car seat, a crib, and outfits for the baby. You may have to purchase a bigger vehicle as your family grows.

However, most parents don't have to buy a conversion van with wheelchair lockdowns, remodel the house to accommodate a power wheelchair, or buy an augmentative communication device for a nonverbal child. If you have a child with a disability, there will be expensive and necessary purchases like these. Health insurance may cover portions, but copays, warranties, and other charges can be expensive.

Sometimes the costs are prohibitive indeed; you simply can't find a way to fund everything. When that happens, you have to face reality and trust in the great job you are doing on your child's behalf. It can be hard to remember what an awesome advocate you really are for your child; there is a temptation to feel inadequate. You can turn to God in prayer for the confidence and affirmation you need to dispel such false ideas.

Envision Jesus looking at you with loving and compassionate eyes. Let yourself feel his love for you. He sees clearly all that you do on behalf of your child. You can trust that Jesus looks with love into your eyes. You can trust him to be an awesome advocate for you.

If you have ever questioned whether you are doing all you can for your child, you are not alone. We have wondered this many times during our autism journey.

When Danielle was in kindergarten, we knew it was time to give her an improved method of communication. Her speech language pathologist recommended that she use an electronic augmentative communication device. It sounded wonderful until we learned that the price tag was seven thousand dollars. That is a lot of money to take from a family's budget! Yet we knew it would help Danielle make great progress in all areas of her life.

We wondered if our health insurance would cover the cost. The policy contained a provision for such a device if it was medically necessary. Danielle was unable to speak, so we thought it would be easy to prove that the machine was necessary. We were astounded when the insurance company denied the claim on the grounds that Danielle *might* develop speech one day!

We were granted a hearing before the insurance company. A panel of professionals sat on one side of the conference room table, while we sat with Danielle on the other side. At one point, we invited the pediatrician on the panel to ask Danielle anything he wanted to know. He turned to her and asked her to tell him her name and her age.

Danielle sat there in complete silence, looking very sweet in her summer dress and pigtails. The members of the panel looked at each other and sighed. We left there smiling, with the claim stamped "APPROVED" and whispering a soulful "Thank you, Jesus!"

This was an important victory for us. In a short time, the machine arrived on our doorstep, and Danielle's world opened up. Even now, seeing her make her way through the screens to find icons and construct sentences is inspiring. She has "her voice"! It's hard to imagine her communicating any other way. We can honestly say it was worth all the energy, all the time, all the fight, and all the prayer.

Struggles and Sacrifice

We can only imagine the financial strain that families with children with more complex physical and medical needs face. When you are talking about customized wheelchairs, lifts, hospital beds, expensive medications, prostheses, and physical remodeling of your home to make it accessible, the costs can seem astronomical!

Families may have to make sacrifices with regard to work, career choices, and household budgets. It may be difficult for each parent to hold a full-time or even a part-time job, depending on the severity of the child's disability. Financial challenges impact the entire family. We knew our three other children would eventually head to college, and we needed to prepare for that.

We have heard many stories from friends and acquaintances about how raising children with special needs has impacted their work lives, career choices, and family dynamics. Some have had to radically change their professions so that they could be more available to their special needs child. Some have lived on far less income than their education, training, and credentials would merit.

Our family's sacrifice involved Mercedes working part-time at a lower level of responsibility than she was qualified for and with much less pay. This job allowed flexibility in her hours and time off when it was needed. We were fortunate that David's salary as a physical therapist allowed us to do this.

For your family, the financial hardship may be severe and even seem overwhelming. An important point to remember is that prayer can help you make the decisions that are right for your family. We have learned that prayer makes a difference. We do our best with our human resources, we pray often, and we leave the rest to God.

Cultivating Gratitude

When we look back over the years, we can see how the hand of God was directing our career steps in ways we never could have imagined. Having a child with special needs has led Mercedes to reach out with greater compassion toward the students in her classroom. In this way, Danielle's autism feels like a gift, as it has enabled Mercedes to see how a student's disability affects their learning and behavior. This helps Mercedes respond more appropriately to students and provide proper modifications for them.

Likewise David was led from geriatric physical therapy to developmental and pediatric physical therapy. When he looks at his patients, he often sees Danielle in them. This empowers him to treat his patients with the dignity and respect that they deserve. Having a child with special needs has fueled his interest in working with these populations and has led to greater professional development. This has made him a better physical therapist and a more compassionate person than he probably would have been.

God's plans for us to use our talents unfolded in ways we did not expect. We have been able to share our experiences as authors and speakers. We marvel that God has allowed us to use our time, talent, and education in this way. This positive perspective on our circumstances developed over time.

We see God's grace at work in our family life, especially in the positive contributions that Danielle has made in our lives and in the lives of others. We look back with a sense of gratitude that God is at the helm. He helps us weather the storms and appreciate the fair skies that follow.

Prayer can cultivate gratitude. It can help us realize that life is a journey to where we want to go but also to places that are not on our itinerary. These places may be dry and hard, like a desert, but we can find a stark beauty there, a ruggedness that leads us to reconcile hardship with beauty.

Perhaps, in a hard place, you realize that your whole life has been moving toward this moment, that God has brought you here for a reason. You might grow deep roots in the desert pavement, because the water underneath nourishes the little cactus flower of your soul. You thank God for bringing you here, where you did not know there was water. God knew.

So find a quiet place—perhaps first thing in the morning, but any time will do. Sit comfortably, and thank God for the opportunity to be with him this day in prayer. Look around, and give thanks for this moment of peace and calm. Breathe in, and say to yourself, "I thank you for guiding me to places I would not have gone." Breathe out, and say, "Thank you for allowing me to journey with you."

Allow your gratitude to move outward, toward your family and close relationships. Breathing in, "I thank you for my family and the opportunity to love them and be loved by them." Breathing out, "I thank you for allowing me to journey with you."

Project your gratitude even further out, perhaps to your workplace. Breathing in, "I thank you for my job and the chance to model your love and healing presence as I provide for my family's needs." Breathing out, "I thank you for allowing me to journey with you."

Continue to express your gratitude for successively wider blessings. Remember to breathe in thanking God for the specific blessing and breathe out thanking him for the gift of journeying with him. Praying like this on a regular basis will help you develop a sense of gratitude for all that God has done and is doing in your life.

Not Even Solomon in All His Glory

When you are caught in the middle of financial challenges, things can seem pretty bleak. Financial strain is a real downer. It can sap your energy and leave you feeling hopeless and bitter. You might find it hard to concentrate or discern solutions. Your marriage can deteriorate. Your patience with the kids can wear thin, and your temper can flare. These challenges can spill into your job, and problems at work can lead to more financial worries.

We can turn with confidence to our loving Father. How do we do this? One good way is to select a passage from the Bible and visualize ourselves in the scene. Try this out using the following passage from the Gospel according to St. Matthew. Jesus is speaking to the crowds that have gathered:

Therefore I tell you, do not worry about your life, what you will eat or what you will drink, or about your body, what you will wear. Is not life more than food, and the body more than clothing? Look at the birds of the air; they neither sow nor reap nor gather into barns, and yet your heavenly Father feeds them. Are you not of more value than they? And can any of you by worrying add a single hour to your span of life? And why do you worry about clothing? Consider the lilies of the field, how they grow; they neither toil nor spin, yet I tell you, even Solomon in all his glory was not clothed like one of these. But if God so clothes the grass of the field, which is alive today and tomorrow is thrown into the oven, will he not much more clothe you—you of little faith? Therefore do not worry, saying, "What will we eat?" or "What will we drink?" or "What will we wear?" For it is the Gentiles who strive for all these things; and indeed your heavenly Father knows that you need all these things. But strive first for the kingdom of God and his righteousness, and all these things will be given to you as well.

So do not worry about tomorrow, for tomorrow will bring worries of its own. Today's trouble is enough for today. (Matthew 6:25-34)

Now put yourself in the story. Picture yourself and your family sitting on a homespun blanket or reed mat. You are hungry for spiritual nourishment. And that's not all you're hungry for. You, like most of the crowd who have gathered to hear this young rabbi, are poor laborers. You wonder if you have enough money to properly care for your disabled child and to buy some fish or chickpea flour at the end of the day. And this rabbi has just told you that such worries are unproductive and even get in the way of your spiritual growth and development. You look at Jesus, and perhaps you roll your eyes derisively and think, "Great, more pie in the sky!"

But then you glance at the wild flowers growing from the rocky soil, and you think hard about his words. You can see that, for Jesus, it's not about pie in the sky; it's about having the faith to wake up another day and do the things you need to do to carry on. It's about placing enough trust in God's providence that you stick it out and don't give up. You see the truth in what this young rabbi is saying.

Worry can paralyze us. It doesn't pay the bills. But hope and trust in the God who provides gives us strength to act in the here and now. It can empower us to attend to practical considerations and also to confront unfair economic, political, and social structures that need to be addressed. It renews our confidence, and then we find positive things happening. God does provide!

Questions

1. What career choices and financial sacrifices have you made due to your child's special needs?
2. Think about how you have experienced God's presence in your life during your special needs journey. How have you felt God's guidance and compassion?
3. How do worries about money and finances affect your spiritual life? How do they affect your prayer?

Giving Thanks
Is One Way to Pray

When we view our lives through the lens of faith, we see God's grace unfold, even when we struggle and can't find answers. Faith gives us space to live in the questions and ambiguities in which we find ourselves, to move through the struggles and sacrifices we cannot avoid. It grants us perspective on the purpose and meaning of the struggles, so we can see their value.

Faith lets us see the gift of our child with special needs and to respond authentically with gratitude. Thanking God is one of the most important things we can do. In thanking him, we embrace our lives and energize our souls. Prayers of gratitude are grounded in the recognition that God has allowed us to journey with him to places we would not have gone but where we most needed to go.

Lord, you know what we need before we know ourselves. Help us trust that you will provide us with the material things we need and allow us to pursue meaningful employment that makes the most of our education, talents, and abilities. We ask for the opportunity to work at something we love that leads to prosperity. Let this work fit into our lives and not conflict with our need to care for our special needs son or daughter. When we have to make sacrifices, let these lead to personal insight and discovery. Let us grow from the experience of raising a child with special needs, so that we become better at what we do, more caring, and more competent. Help us mirror your love and boundless mercy to those we work with and serve.

Help us to know, dear God, that financial sacrifices allow us to deepen our trust in you alone. Place gratitude in our hearts, helping us see and appreciate all our blessings, especially the gift of our children. Help us not confuse material things with the relationships that truly matter.

Help us fight for the things our child needs. Put the right words in our mouths when we stand before insurance companies, school districts, and government agencies to obtain necessary equipment and resources to advance our child's life. Help us generate the energy we need, and help us stick with each struggle to the end.

Lord, replace our worries and anxieties with confidence and the strength each day to carry on.

Chapter Seven

Activities of Daily Living and Travel

Our family, friends, and acquaintances are surprised sometimes by how much we need to help Danielle each day. She is well into her teenage years, and some people take it for granted that a kid her age would be independent with such things as dressing, bathing, and brushing her teeth. However, while Danielle has made much progress in all of these areas, she still needs our daily help. For example, she brushes her own teeth, but we need to be close by to ensure that she does a thorough job.

When it comes to dressing herself, Danielle does not recognize what to wear for different types of weather and different occasions. She might put her clothing on inside out or put a shoe on the wrong foot. She needs help to fix these things.

Helping Danielle has become a normal part of our family's day. Her siblings pitch in to remind her of things and to help her. They do it lovingly, but there are days when we wish it was not necessary. There are times when we wish we could get a day off from caretaking.

Still, we are grateful for all the progress Danielle has made. And we recognize that other families deal with similar concerns, and many provide a much higher level of care. Just yesterday at Mass, we saw a child who had a tracheotomy. His family provides a very high level of care just so he can breathe properly.

They must keep the trach clean and his airway clear. They must monitor how much oxygen is left in the canister and provide a new tank when needed. They must do this every day. That is a lot of care.

Being able to walk independently is another activity of daily life (ADL). Some parents help their child maneuver through their environment by pushing a wheelchair, providing a handhold to steady them, or even carrying them. A family from our parish used to carry their adult son up to receive Holy Communion each week. That is heroic!

Our Lady, Undoer of Knots

Parents of children with special needs have no shortage of things to pray for when it comes to ADLs. You can pray that your child learn how to perform tasks more independently. Ask God to help your child progress through the various stages of dressing themselves.

For example, you can pray for their ability to put on shoes when the laces are made loose and the shoes are presented for one foot at a time. Then ask God that your child be able to manipulate the shoes by themselves, putting the shoes on the correct feet and, if possible, learning to tie them. Do the same with putting on clothing and brushing teeth.

You could feel overwhelmed by all the things your child has to learn to do, all the different steps that he or she must master on the way to greater independence. How do you present your petitions to God in a heartfelt way? How do you express your hopes and dreams?

One good way is to give them to Mary under the title Our Lady, Undoer of Knots. You can think of the stages toward your child's independence as a series of knots that need to be untied.

We first heard of this favorite devotion of Pope Francis when he came to Philadelphia. The coordinators of the visit constructed a grotto outside the cathedral, using long strips of white paper on which the faithful had written their prayer petitions. These strips were fastened to frames to form a large hut, as well as to railings and iron fence posts. Stepping into the grotto, we felt as if we were covered with prayer.

You can create your own grotto in your home. You will need long strips of plain white paper and a magic marker. Think about different activities of daily living and the parts of each that your child needs help with. Write these as individual prayer petitions, one on each paper strip. You and your family can fasten these strips to appropriate places, such as to the stairway bannister, the armrests of chairs, or wherever you think best. If you are good at this sort of thing, you can create frames to which you can attach the prayers and form a hut or other structure.

If you have a statue of Mary, then consider placing the prayer petitions over or near the statue, in any way that is reverent and appropriate. Or you can attach the prayer strips to a crucifix on the wall, so that they hang from Jesus' outstretched arms.

Each day untie one or more of these petitions, and recite the prayers to Mary, Undoer of Knots, which are available on the Internet. Ask her to intercede before her beloved son on your behalf. As your child masters parts of the ADLs, remember to thank Mary for her help in untying these knots in your child's life.

Clean Up, Aisle Four

Being able to function appropriately in the community is another part of daily living that children with special needs face. A few years ago, taking Danielle to a store, especially a grocery store, was a huge challenge. She would dart over to the salad bar and try to help herself to items there, even very hot entrees with steam coming from them. She would try to eat the ice surrounding fresh fish. We never knew what she was going to do.

One time we rounded a corner to find a large display of small candies on an endcap. Danielle grabbed a bag and ripped it open. Candies flew all over the floor. An elderly couple was coming down the aisle, and we hurried to clean up the mess so that the couple would not fall. While we were doing this, Danielle grabbed another bag and ripped it open. Luckily no one was hurt, but it was a while before we dared to take Danielle back to that store.

As she got older, Danielle learned more about what was appropriate and what was not. She still requires a high level of supervision. But our hearts are not thumping each time we enter a store with her.

Taking Danielle out to a restaurant was equally difficult. She had a hard time waiting for her food to come. If a waitress was coming by with a full plate of food, Danielle would attempt to grab the French fries right off the tray. She did not understand the social ramifications of taking other people's food; she just knew she was hungry and liked what she saw.

When this happened, we would be embarrassed and apologetic. Our kids would be embarrassed too. One time we apologized to a woman who told us she understood entirely. Her grandson had been diagnosed with autism the week before. We felt a familiar comradery, as we often did when talking to families of children with special needs.

Taking your child out in the community can be a scary thing, but it is crucial to your child's development and your family's well-being. Pray for your child's success in community interactions, that he or she have the necessary behavioral skills, impulse control, and ability to function in unstructured environments. Ask God that your child develop a sense of context, the understanding that there is a difference between what is appropriate behavior in the community and what is allotwed at home or in school. Pray for your child to feel comfortable, calm, and competent, even when things are open, unpredictable, and unfamiliar.

Don't forget to pray for yourself and your other family members. You may feel isolated and shut off from the community of other adults; ask God to heal these feelings. Ask him to restore your sense of connection to your peers.

Pray for the strength and courage to get out there. Ask for renewed confidence in community interactions. Pray for your community, that it can be a place where others can see God at work in your special needs child and can experience compassion and mercy.

Travel

Many people attribute to St. Augustine the quote, "The world is a book, and those who do not travel read only one page." Travel can be fun, but it can also be hard, especially if there are delays, noise, crowds, and chaos. It can be exhilarating and fatiguing at the same time. Parents of children with special needs often have particular trouble traveling.

Recently our entire family was traveling by air, and Danielle was randomly pulled aside and searched as we were going through security at the airport. Talk about an unfriendly autism encounter! We always hold Danielle's hand in crowded public places, so that she does not get separated from us. When she was pulled aside and we were told to wait in another line, this was frightening, not only to her but to us. She doesn't always respond well to people she doesn't know, and she doesn't always follow commands easily.

It was a mess. The airport was super crowded, our shoes were off, we were trying to keep our eyes on our personal items going through the scanner, and Danielle was separated from us. Fortunately, once we got on the plane, things went better than we expected. We were grateful for the easy flight.

Travel by plane poses challenges to children who use wheelchairs. Aircraft are not really handicapped accessible. The aisles are narrow, so it is hard to bring your child aboard, not to mention handle your family's luggage. It can be difficult for your child to get in and out of the seat. Restrooms are next to impossible. And when you arrive at your destination, you may have problems getting a rental vehicle that can accommodate a wheelchair.

Vacations by their very nature involve changes from ordinary routines, and this can prove challenging for children. You stay in different places, often driving a different car, watching television shows on different channels, eating different foods, and doing different activities. There can be long lines and lots of waiting. You may underestimate how much time activities as well as driving to and from will take.

Some kids have increased anxiety due to all of this, and behavioral issues may pop up. Parents can get pretty frazzled too! Sometimes it doesn't feel much like a vacation.

Perhaps your family is about to take a trip. While you may feel excited, you also may feel anxious about the logistics of it all. You may be worried about your child tolerating crowds on the highway or in an airport. This is a good opportunity to pause, take a few breaths, and remember that God is with you on your journey.

Traveling with Faith

Let's turn to St. Christopher, the patron saint of travelers, and seek inspiration from his story. He stands as an example of how helping others allows us to encounter Christ.

One of the many legends surrounding St. Christopher tells how he used to carry travelers across a fierce river. One day a small child asked Christopher to take him across. The water was especially fast and dangerous that day, but the saint hoisted the child up and placed him on his own aging but still burly shoulders. Cautiously he set foot into the rapids.

Christopher felt an increasingly great weight pushing down as he walked. It felt as if he carried the full weight of the world, with all its suffering and sin, on his back and shoulders. A foot nearly slipped on one of the pebbles that dotted the bottom of the fast-moving river, but he held fast to the child and recovered his balance. The child clung to his neck and beard.

Christopher made his way toward the opposite bank. He did not allow the growing heaviness to defeat him but instead drew strength from it. As he approached the other side, he could hear the rustling of leaves on the trees that grew there. The sound reached deep into Christopher's soul, and he smiled.

A few more steps, and at last he set the child down on the other bank. He knew in his heart that the young traveler he had just carried was the Christ child. He had walked with Christ on his shoulders, carrying with him the full weight of the world! Christopher was forever changed and strengthened by this experience.

Prayer is a type of travel. When we pray, our hearts and minds travel to the very dwelling place of God. We can think of this as a slow and timeless journey from our ordinary world down a river with loops and bends into sacred time and space. Once we experience this river, even if for only a moment, it changes our lives. Only when we set foot in the water and embark on the journey can we experience the new life to which we are called.

To understand this better, let's turn to another faithful servant of God and to another river. In the Book of Exodus, we meet Jochebed, the mother of Moses. She has just given birth to her son, whom we know is destined to free the children of Israel from cruel slavery in Egypt. However, Pharaoh has ordered the death of all newborn Hebrew boys, and Jochebed must find a way to save her child's life.

With the help of her daughter Miriam, Jochebed places the baby in a papyrus basket, which she sets among the reeds on the bank of the Nile. The basket sits exactly where God wants Moses to be found (see Exodus 2:1-10).

Parenting a child with special needs involves risk. In prayer we can watch over our children just as Miriam guarded her little brother down by the river. We can see our children come safely to the heart of God.

Sometimes it may seem easier to collapse your world, to limit your horizons in order to avoid possible failures. We have seen parents become so worn down and discouraged that they no longer risk travel or going out. They rarely expose their children to new situations and experiences. They may become so reliant on routines that they are afraid to deviate from them. Visiting family members, attending a wedding, or traveling on an airplane seem like too much. Families become isolated, and the children have little opportunity to develop competency in new areas.

This is a strategy based on fear. It may be safe, but it's unfulfilling and ultimately unsustainable.

In the beginning of our family's journey with autism, we were pulled in this direction. We found ourselves avoiding difficult activities and occasions, including community and family events. We became wary of travel. It was a very painful time for us. Fortunately, with the help of prayer, we realized that we were collapsing Danielle's world.

Prayer also helped us entrust our journeys to God and take risks. It helped us learn how to be brave and faith-filled, for the good of all our children and our own good too. Prayer allowed us to take the risk that St. Christopher took when he carried the Christ child. It allowed us to take the risk that Jochebed took when she set the baby Moses on the bank of the Nile.

Questions

1. In what ways can helping your child perform tasks and activities become a prayerful activity for you? How can it lead you closer to God instead of distracting you?
2. What knots in your life would you like to see untied? Why do you think people turn to Mary to undo the knots in their lives?
3. How can we see prayer as a type of travel? For you, does it resemble a long and winding journey down a river or travel by jet plane? How does prayer lead you toward your destination?

Turning to the Saints
Is One Way to Pray

Veneration of saints and turning to them for guidance and intercession are ancient practices in the Church. We can read about the saints' lives and find in them storehouses of inspiration. The saints model how God acts in human beings, to draw us toward deep communion with him.

Saints are our faith ancestors, upon whom we can rely in our own struggles. We can draw near them in prayer and receive their wisdom. Their stories can become our stories, as we encounter them in our hearts and ride on the same divine energy that powers them.

Familiarize yourself with the saints by reading about them and viewing stained-glass windows, paintings, sculptures, films, and plays about their lives. Then choose a saint whose story and special qualities inspire you. Appreciate these qualities, and experience them in yourself. Allow the saint's connectedness to God to draw you to the divine. Ask the saint to guide you.

———————————┼———————————

Dear God, we come to you, asking that our children learn how to successfully perform their activities of daily living to the best of their abilities. We carry with us the hope of a bright future, one in which our children develop competence and independence in all areas, so that they may lead happy, fulfilling, and productive lives. Grant to our children the joy of mastering such skills as dressing, bathing, feeding, toileting, hygiene, and mobility. Allow us to see the thrill of accomplishment on our children's faces as they successfully tie their shoelaces, button or zip their jackets, and comb their own hair. May we see our children rise from a chair and walk without assistance.

There is much for our children to learn. When they can't perform a task by themselves, allow us to be there to help as much as is needed. May we see steady progress: our children advancing even as we learn to accept those things that they are unable to do.

Life is a tangle of knots that we struggle to untie. On our own, we can only go so far. Help us realize that we can call on Our Blessed Mother Mary to undo the knots for us. Help us enter her grotto, where she unties each knot with which our children struggle.

May we realize the importance of community as a place of opportunity and learning for our family. Help us not retreat into isolation or feel the need to shield our children from the challenges that lie outside our little realm. Help us negotiate such challenges, that our children may grow in their ability to access and enjoy the various communities to which they belong. Help these communities recognize the dignity inherent in our children and see in them the marvelous unfolding of your will, O Lord.

Create in our children and in us a love of travel and adventure, so that we may more fully experience the world you have created. Help us overcome the challenges of traveling by train, plane, or automobile. May everything go smoothly in our travels. May our family get to our destinations safely and in an enjoyable, stress-free way.

May our children with special needs adapt to new sights, new sounds, and new places. May travel open up new horizons and new dreams. May it create in us a new heart!

May we, like St. Christopher, hoist our children high onto our shoulders as we step into the bracing waters of life! Give us the strength and the courage to keep going, the sure-footedness to stay upright, and the endurance to reach the other side. Allow us to be transformed by the experience.

May we learn to discover you, O Lord, in prayer. May our minds and hearts come to dwell in you, now and forever. Amen!

Chapter Eight
Praying for Your Child's Social Success

Parents want their children to have happy and engaging social lives. However, when children do not understand how to develop friendships or even how to have appropriate interactions with others, they may have a hard time achieving this.

Disabilities such as autism impact a child's awareness of what is appropriate social behavior. Such children may be less aware of social cues, personal space, and hygiene. Often they maintain limited eye contact. And there can be language deficits that make conversation frustrating and difficult. Kids may become objects of bullying and ridicule and not even be aware of this.

Sometimes when people greet Danielle and attempt to speak to her, Danielle does not respond or even look at them. It's understandable that someone may misconstrue this as disinterest or even rudeness. Yet this is far from the truth. Danielle enjoys interacting with others. She sometimes just needs cues and prompts from us in order to direct her attention to the other person..

Children with autism and other disabilities want to engage others and be part of the fun. They may be neurologically ill-prepared to handle social information, however.

Mind Your Manners

Parents try to instill a sense of manners in their children from an early age. Knowing manners is necessary when it comes to successful interactions with others. Saying thank you to the person who helps you in school, at home, or in the community can go a long way toward fostering and ensuring pleasant interactions.

When our children were very young, *please* and *thank you* were magical words in our house. Like most children, ours learned very early that adding "please" to a sentence made it more likely that they would get what they wanted. Also they learned that when someone said "please" and "thank you" to them, that person respected them. When a child does not understand the magic of these two words, they may find others more resistant to helping them and showing them respect or friendship.

Hello and *goodbye* are also magical words. Knowing how to greet someone and leave them is a basic social skill.

It took a long time for Danielle to acknowledge people in these ways. Even today, these words do not come spontaneously to her. We encourage Danielle to greet her relatives and friends, often prompting her to say hello. When we leave an event, we bring her over to the host and have her say goodbye.

Many children with special needs are verbal. However, they often do not understand the social importance of greeting people and saying goodbye or the importance of a friendly handshake. This can negatively impact their ability to get jobs, maintain friendships, and negotiate relationships.

Don't Stand so Close to Me

Honoring someone's personal space is a social grace that is hard for people with certain disabilities. Many people with autism have no idea that they are standing or sitting too close to someone, perhaps suggesting aggression or defiance and causing unease.

David, a physical therapist, has worked in developmental centers with disabled adults. He remembers a patient who in his zeal to interact and be friendly would try to stand about three inches from David's face. Every time David would take a step backward, the patient would step forward. One time he walked David into a wall. Although David understood why this occurred, it felt threatening.

People who are not aware of this tendency among the disabled may react in negative ways, perceiving physical closeness as an invasion of their personal space. Similarly, getting too close to someone—even accidentally bumping into them or stepping on their foot—requires an acknowledgement and "excuse me." Even people who function in a high range in many areas may act as if nothing has occurred and inadvertently provoke a negative reaction in others.

The problem can extend beyond physical space. Perhaps your child interrupts you when you are speaking to others, making you feel tense and lose your train of thought.

Prayer Is Social

If social interaction is a problem for your child, why not pray about it? You can pray that your child find appropriate times to speak, so there are fewer interruptions. You can ask God to help you respond better to your child, with less annoyance and irritation. And pray that other people understand your child and do not see them as rude or bothersome.

In many ways, our spiritual life as Christians is inherently social. When we pray, we turn our attention to God in three Persons, the Holy Trinity. In prayer we greet the Father, Son, and Holy Spirit. When we prayerfully make the Sign of the Cross, it is a profession of faith but also a form of address.

God has instilled in us a social dimension, a social nature that we carry with us by virtue of being created in his image and likeness. Through this social nature, he engages us. He has opened himself to us by virtue of the great mystery of the Incarnation in Christ Jesus. When we pray, we recognize this mystery and respond to God. We say our hello to God.

We even say please and thank you. Think about it: When we petition God, we ask that he grant our prayer if it is pleasing to him. Authentic prayers of this sort arise from deep within us, and they always begin, "*Please* God, if it be *your* will, . . ." Likewise, in response to God's blessings in our lives, we offer prayers of thanksgiving. As our sense of gratitude matures, we extend our thanks to God as an acknowledgement of his holiness, and this fills us with joy. We pray, "God, thank you for your goodness."

Jesus, by virtue of being both man and God, understood this social aspect of prayer. When asked how we should pray, he gave us the Our Father, which expresses and models the soul's authentic response to God and reliance on divine providence:

Our Father, who art in heaven,
hallowed be thy name.
Thy kingdom come.
Thy will be done
on earth as it is in heaven.
Give us this day our daily bread,
and forgive us our trespasses,
as we forgive those who trespass against us,
and lead us not into temptation,
but deliver us from evil.

When we pray the Our Father or any genuine prayer that rises from our depths, we consciously acknowledge and address the God of the Universe. When we say, "Thy will be done," we align our will with God's. When we add, "For the kingdom, the power, and the glory are yours, now and forever," as we do during the Mass, we thank God for his goodness. When we finish the prayer to return to our ordinary lives, we say our goodbye till next time.

Singing a Litany

You can organize your petitions into a litany, in which you ask a series of saints to pray for your child with special needs. Our Church is the *ekklesia* or assembly, the people of God, and as such is inherently social. Our life as Christians is grounded in community and interaction with other people. The saints represent the highest ideals of our human family, and it is fitting to pray to God through them, especially when asking for your son or daughter with special needs to understand and function in the social domain.

The communion of saints is a good way for us to connect to our God. They have lived lives of love and service to God and neighbor. They are models of how the people of God should treat one another.

It's helpful to remember that many holy men and women devoted their lives to helping people with disabilities and illnesses of all sorts. St. Damien of Molokai comes to mind here. He spent many years working with people with leprosy. He tended to their physical, spiritual, and emotional needs.

This was at a time when many people with leprosy were forced to live in quarantine. Fr. Damien served in a leper colony on the island of Molokai in Hawaii. His ministry among those who were considered social and medical outcasts may resonate with parents and people with special needs today.

Other notable saints associated with people with disabilities include:

- St. Francis de Sales, patron saint of people with hearing impairments;
- St. Lucy, patron saint of people with eye disorders;
- St. Dymphna, patron saint of people with mental illness;
- St. Blaise, patron saint of people with throat ailments (including speech and communication problems);
- St. Raphael the Archangel, patron saint of people with visual and emotional difficulties;
- St. Jude, patron saint of impossible causes;

- St. Philomena, patron saint of children's health;
- St. Luke, patron saint of healing.

You can also include people who are not yet canonized, such as:

- Blessed John Licci, patron of people with head injuries;
- Fr. Henri Nouwen, theologian, advocate, and activist on behalf of people with disabilities.

Pick your favorite saints, and include them in your litany.

Traditionally, litanies are sung in plain chant, similar to the style you sometimes hear during solemn parts of the Mass. They are usually in a call-and-response format. The cantor addresses each saint or group of saints by name, and the people respond, "Pray for us!" The litany begins by invoking God the Father, Son, and Holy Spirit, followed by Holy Mary, Mother of God, and the archangels Michael, Gabriel, and Raphael.

A full litany can be quite lengthy, including patriarchs and prophets, the apostles, Mary Magdalene, the martyrs, bishops and doctors of the church, priests and religious, and laity. You can decide how many saints to include. Most likely you will want to include saints with whom you relate in a special way, such as the saints listed above.

You can sing a litany privately—by yourself or with family members and friends. A litany can also be part of a healing service, a retreat, or another event. It is a wonderful way of offering prayer intentions for your special needs child in the social context of the Church.

A Sweet-Sixteen Party

Last year our daughter Danielle turned sixteen. At this age, many girls have sweet-sixteen parties. Sometimes these can be extravagant social events. We threw a sweet-sixteen party that was simpler but no less a success.

Thankfully, nearly everyone invited was able to come to Danielle's party. Children with disabilities generally have fewer social opportunities than their nondisabled peers. A few of the parents shared how excited their children were to receive an invitation. One mom said that her child had actually been counting down the days until the party. Danielle was equally overjoyed at having her friends there.

A few months later, one of Danielle's classmates had a sweet-sixteen party and invited Danielle. It was heartwarming to see many of the same kids invited for party number two. There were a lot of smiles on their faces that night, as everyone was reunited. One of the girls asked the others to pose with her for "selfies." This was priceless.

One of the fruits of our prayer was being able to stand back that night and watch Danielle be a teenager first and a child with autism second.

Questions

1. Think about an occasion when your son or daughter was excluded or included in a party. How did you feel? How might you turn these feelings over to God?

2. Why did Jesus teach us to pray to God as *our* Father? What are some ways that this relationship with God affects your prayer life?

3. Do you have a favorite saint, one whom you call upon to intercede on your behalf? Invite this saint to intercede for your child's social development and success.

Formulaic Prayer
Is One Way to Pray

In this chapter, we looked at the Our Father, which is an example of a formulaic prayer. These are specific prayers that come to us by way of Scripture or Tradition. There are many such prayers, and they are among the first we learn to pray. They are beneficial prayers that we can go to when we wish to turn to God.

The Our Father, Hail Mary, Hail Holy Queen, Act of Contrition, and Grace Before Meals are so familiar that we may be tempted to rush through them. Try instead to pray the words clearly and carefully. Speak each prayer as if it were for the first time, with full attention and reverence. Listen to the words. Allow them to come from your heart.

Dear God, you created all of us in your divine image and gifted us with a social nature—that we may manifest and experience love among our fellows, as you manifest and experience perfect love in the mystery of the

Holy Trinity. Through the great mystery of the Incarnation, you sent your Son to share our human nature and to walk among us, that in a very real sense we can know that you embrace our humanity from birth to death. In so doing, you have made our breadth of experience holy.

Help our child develop the necessary social skills to form relationships, to enjoy friendship and love, and to draw strength from the community. Help our child maintain appropriate eye contact and respect for the personal space of others. Protect them from bullying and ridicule. Let them acknowledge people by name and show respect for others with proper manners. May they develop a genuine enjoyment for the company of others and show appropriate love and concern.

Help our child feel that they fit in with their peers. May they be invited to participate in healthy and wholesome activities, such as chaperoned parties and dances. May they encounter good friends at these events. Dear God, see to it that everyone has a great time!

Holy Mary, Mother of God, pray for us.

St. Joseph, her spouse, pray for us.

Saints Michael, Gabriel, and Raphael, pray for us.

St. Jude, pray for us.

St. Mary Magdalene, pray for us.

Saints Luke, Blaise, Dymphna, Lucy, and Philomena, pray for us.

Saints Frances de Sales and Damien of Molokai, Blessed John Licci, and Fr. Henri Nouwen, pray for us.

All the faithful departed, pray for us.

CHAPTER NINE

When the School Bus Stops Coming

This chapter explores your child's transition into adulthood, rites of passage along the way, and what will happen when you are no longer there to care for him or her. Concern about these matters is often in the back of a special needs parent's mind; it can feel like a deep weight dragging you down.

There is a natural fear of the unknown and a nagging awareness that, despite all you do to lay the groundwork for your child's future, so much lies outside your control. However, this lack of control can call forth and fuel an authentic faith response. Prayer can be a powerful and transformative expression of this faith.

A Bittersweet Rite of Passage

Rites of passage are many. Such events are important because they mark time and memorialize a child's transformation into an adult. They impact the child but also their parents and their community. They take us back to our own adolescence and early adulthood.

Getting a driver's license is perhaps the most anticipated rite of passage in the life of a teenager. In our state, you can get your driver's license at age seventeen. When our sons turned seventeen, we were busy helping them learn how to parallel park. Or we were sweating it out in the passenger seat, our hearts skipping with every left turn. When our boys passed their road tests, we celebrated with photographs of them sporting their new license.

Danielle's seventeenth birthday was different; it was bittersweet. For our newest seventeen-year-old, there would be no car keys and no driver's license. How could there be? We did mark the day with a trip to the State Division of Motor Vehicles. Instead of going there for Danielle's road test, we went to get her "nondriver ID." It looks very much like a driver's license with one crucial difference: it doesn't authorize the person to drive. It does not say "driver's license" anywhere on it.

We were unprepared when the clerk asked if we wanted Danielle's ID to state that she was willing to be an organ donor. Since Danielle is nonverbal, this decision fell to us. We felt uneasy making this decision for her. Our sons had answered the organ donor question on their own, filling out the form independently and checking boxes as they saw fit.

In a way, this brought us back to the day when Danielle was diagnosed with autism. Even then we knew that one day she would turn seventeen, but she could never sit behind the steering wheel of a moving car. Though this was years away, the thought was painful. It was no less so when the day actually came.

The day was bittersweet because we were happy to celebrate Danielle's birthday but also sad to see another dramatic difference between Danielle, her siblings, and other kids her age. Fortunately our sad thoughts were fleeting, as we realized how much Danielle brought to our lives. And she was happy to have her very own ID, albeit a nondriver one. The whole family celebrated with her.

We know that, as Danielle moves toward adulthood, there will be many rites of passage. They may bring us twinges of sadness or even gushes of tears, but we know they are simply parts of the great unfolding of God's grace in our lives.

The Special Needs Prom

Who doesn't remember their high school prom? Most people look back on theirs with nostalgia, remembering those carefree younger days. There are many things about this rite of passage that make it hard for kids with special needs.

Proms are social events, so kids who have trouble with social interactions can find them overwhelming. They are usually crowded and noisy, and the acoustics may cause problems. Lighting can be too dim, too bright, or both. There can be strobe lights, which are problematic for children with seizure disorders. Formal attire is required. Updos, manicured nails, high heels, ties, and other fashion adornments can seem strange and uncomfortable.

We were delighted when we found out that Danielle's school offered a special needs prom. It had all the trimmings of a traditional prom but on a scale that was manageable for Danielle and her classmates. Danielle felt like a princess with her manicure, fancy hairstyle, beautiful dress, and sparkling shoes. We were thrilled to see her so happy.

We knew that Danielle would be well supervised at the prom, since her teacher and aides would be there to help out. The paparazzi of happy parents was in full force, snapping photos at the promenade before the kids entered the ballroom for an enchanted evening. When we returned later to pick up Danielle, we could feel the fun and excitement in the banquet room and see the joy on all the kids' faces. We felt renewed in body and soul. We wanted to dance too.

Sometimes parents of children with special needs fall into the habit of only seeing the challenges and seeing the struggles. They can forget how much happiness there is in life. To see their child so thoroughly enjoying themselves makes life worth living.

Joy is an important part of life. Pay attention to it, and allow yourself to feel it percolate through you. Do not miss it! Let your joy be a spontaneous occasion for prayer. Like the psalmist, beat out praise and thanksgiving with your feet and hands.

Praise him with trumpet sound;
    praise him with lute and harp!
Praise him with tambourine and dance;
    praise him with strings and pipe!
Praise him with clanging cymbals;
    praise him with loud clashing cymbals!
Let everything that breathes praise the LORD!
Praise the LORD! (Psalm 150:3-6)

College

College is a feasible option for many kids with special needs. This depends, of course, on the characteristics and abilities of the individual child.

When Danielle was initially diagnosed with autism, back in preschool, the child-study team asked us to develop a long-term educational goal for her. We told them that we wanted her to get a college degree. At that time, we did not understand the full impact of Danielle's disability. It took a long time to accept the fact that college would not be a part of her life. It challenged our expectations for her.

Danielle is now at the age when her nondisabled peers are touring colleges, writing college essays, and receiving college acceptances. While we are happy for the successes that other children are experiencing, sometimes we feel sad that our child's path is different from what we had assumed and hoped for when she was born. Maybe this describes your situation too.

This will not be the case for all children with special needs. Many are able to go to college successfully. Children with medical issues such as tracheotomies, physical impairments, and diabetes can come to this milestone, given proper modifications and planning. Still, attending college can be an enormous source of concern for the child and the parents.

Often parents know the types of accommodations that will be necessary for their child's college success. As a physical therapist, David worked with a patient who wanted to attend a local college after high school graduation. This young man had cerebral palsy and had only recently developed the ability to get around his high school with platform crutches instead of a wheelchair. He and his parents were worried that getting around the large college campus on foot would be too much for him. They struggled with whether he should use his wheelchair instead. Considerable care, thought, and prayer went into their decision to try the crutches.

Decisions such as this can be a source of great anxiety for all involved, so don't hesitate to place your concerns in God's hands. You can begin your prayer by recalling that God has created your child as a unique and special individual with purpose and dignity. In Jeremiah 1:5 we hear:

> Before I formed you in the womb, I knew you
> and before you were born I consecrated you.

When you feel anxious about your child's ability to transition to the next step, repeat these words softly to yourself. Remember that God has a plan for your child. Trust in that plan.

Employment

Everyone likes to get a paycheck. In addition, having a job promotes a sense of accomplishment and satisfaction. It allows you to meet new people, have regular social interactions, and utilize your skills and talents, as well as giving you the monetary means to support yourself.

For a child with special needs, finding an appropriate job is not always easy. There are many variables, such as the independence level of the child. This can be a heavy weight on parents and child alike. In addition, some kids may have difficulty keeping the job, learning appropriate work behaviors, advocating for themselves, and learning how to fit in. It is important that people with special needs be in an environment where they find understanding and acceptance.

It is your child's future you are concerned about, and there is a lot at stake. It is not always a situation that is resolved quickly; you might once again find yourself in a challenging situation for the long count. Things might work out to a degree but not be quite satisfactory.

Your child might get a part-time job instead of a full-time one. Perhaps they will be underemployed, at a job that does not fully use their skills or education. There may be concerns about your child's safety on a job, where workers are expected to function at an independent level.

All these issues can be draining and can affect your child's self-esteem. It is hard enough for the nondisabled to be out of work or underemployed. When you have a disability, this can be harder and weigh more heavily on the person and on the parents.

If you share some of these worries about your child's employment, call on St. Joseph, the patron saint of workers. Ask him to intercede for your child to find meaningful and productive employment commensurate with their education, financial needs, and interests. Ask him to protect your child at work. Ask that your child be treated with fairness, dignity, and respect.

Praying for Endurance

It can seem as if you've come a long way and fought many battles on behalf of your child, yet you find yourself back at square one. You feel burned out, unable to carry even one more burden. You can't imagine holding up to one more setback, one more failure, or one more night lying awake.

The cumulative effect of a prolonged struggle can be a dark night in your soul. You may find it hard to pray or access your own heart with words. What you're carrying can feel best borne in silence. It may cook awhile as you sit stone-faced and grim.

Disturbing images may enter your dreams and trouble your sleep. When you try to approach God in prayer and communicate these feelings, you may feel as if you're lowering a bucket into a well with a long rope, only to pull it back and find nothing inside but dry sand.

You may find a parallel between the dryness you feel and how the disciples might have felt the day after Christ's crucifixion. Imagine you are there with them now. You sit in the upper room, with the door locked and windows shuttered. Every time you swallow, you feel a painful lump in your throat. You doubt this sorrow will ever pass.

The next day, you walk numbly into the morning chill, carrying myrrh and your grief to the tomb. An inane monologue runs through your head as you walk. You're tired, and the only thing you can think to say is "Who will roll away the stone for us from the entrance to the tomb?" (Mark 16:3).

Imagine if you had stopped and never walked all the way to the tomb. Think of what you would have missed if you had said to yourself, "What good is all of this? I'm only going through the motions." You would not have seen an empty tomb with the stone rolled away. You would not have heard a young man in white announce, "He is not here. He is risen!"

Imagine you turned away only a mile from your destination. Thank God you dug your sandals into the ground instead and hurried to the tomb.

Fortunately for us, Danielle is a happy teenager. She adapts easily to her surroundings and is flexible when we need to go somewhere. Most days she shows us she is happy by laughing and smiling. It is a rare day when Danielle is not happy.

But those rare days are the worst. They are the days when we can lose our sense of hope. We might worry about the day when we are older and no longer able to care for her—and after that, no longer here on earth to care for her. We can find ourselves conversing with God in a seemingly endless loop of negative thoughts:

- Why me, dear God?
- I can't do this, Lord.
- We are getting too old for this.
- Enough is enough is enough, already!

At such a time, we find it good to reflect on all the progress that Danielle has made. We have witnessed gains that some might think small but that we know are nothing short of miraculous.

Planning Ahead

Still, we worry about some specifics. After the magical age of twenty-one comes and the school's responsibility ends, then what?

- What will my child do during the day?
- Will learning end?
- Will progress end?
- Will there be a successful transition to a new schedule?
- Will my child be bored?
- Will her days be fulfilling?
- Will she still have connections to others?
- Will she have meaningful work?

- Will she be properly cared for?
- Will she be kept safe?
- Will behaviors reemerge once her routine has changed?
- Will people be kind to her?
- Will she be treated with dignity?

These are real worries.

Finding a beneficial day or work program can be a challenge. When the school bus stops coming to your house, your schedule might have to change, or you might need to find an appropriate caretaker. Even if your child is able to take van transportation, the hours might not coincide with your work schedule or the program schedule. We have heard that some adult day programs run for only a few hours a day, around the midmorning to early afternoon hours. This is not often conducive to a parent's work schedule; adjustments may have to be made.

Your child has been in a school setting, where you could be reasonably certain there was sufficient staff keeping an eye out for their safety and meeting their needs. You hope an adult day program has this level of care. Even if that is the case, it can be nerve-wracking to entrust your child's care to a whole new set of people and get familiar with how a program runs.

When your child turns eighteen, you may need to petition for guardianship. This can involve court appearances in front of a judge, who will determine if you (the parent!) are fit for this role. Many questions can flood your mind:

- Do I need to be a full guardian for my child?
- Should I be a limited guardian for my child?

- Whom will I assign as a successor guardian?
- Who will care for my child after I am gone? Will that person feel burdened?
- Where will my child live?

Finally, at some point, you and your spouse will die. It is natural and helpful for people to plan for this with their families. And when you are the parent of a child with special needs, provisions for the future have to be rock solid. They can also be complicated.

There are considerations related to estate planning and wills that are specific to persons with disabilities. Your will may include a special needs trust provision.

Parents must find answers to questions about their child's future, based on the child's strengths and abilities. You might go over these questions in your head every way you can. You might lie awake at night, wondering if you are making the correct decisions for your child. Once again, the best way to proceed is to pray.

Praying the Rosary

Praying the Rosary is a great way to sort out everything that's on your mind and help you clearly assess the choices available for your child. Fingering the beads and repeating the familiar prayers allow you to break up worrisome thoughts that may be playing in your head. The Rosary puts you in touch with God the Father and Mary the Blessed Mother, who together loved and supported Jesus more than anyone else could. Putting your child in their care is an act of love and holy surrender!

And let's not forget the importance of meditating on the mysteries of the Rosary. Focusing on the joyous, luminous, sorrowful, and glorious mysteries in the lives of Jesus and Mary reminds us that each of our lives involves joys and sorrows. Contemplating the deep mysteries of our lives, including having a child with a significant disability, allows us to embrace the God who underlies all of life. We see in the mysteries how the sorrows of life ultimately give way to God's grace and glory.

Apply the mysteries of the Rosary in your own life. As an example, start with the first joyful mystery, the annunciation. Meditate on the angel's announcement to Mary that she was to have a baby boy named Jesus. Try to recall when you first found out you were going to have your child. Think of how happy you felt with this news and the life you envisioned for your child.

We imagine that Mary may have envisioned a certain life for her son. However, one of the great mysteries of life is that it doesn't unfold according to our expectations and ideas. In the annunciation, there is not only the promise of life for Jesus but also the implicit prophecy of the sufferings that he and Mary will endure.

We see the beginning of life as a joyous event, even though we know that life involves suffering too. The Rosary gives us space to explore and experience this in the context of our Christian story. This can be very liberating.

Handing Things over to God

Parenting a child with special needs is all about learning to step back from fear so that you can trust that you have done what you were able to do and that God will take it from there. Ultimately your prayer life cultivates this deep trust. It's important to lay the foundation of being attentive to the love of God and look at the ways this love has unfolded in your life. You can set aside some time each day to just sit and reflect on how God calls you to trust him with all areas of your life.

Find a comfortable spot—either early, before others in your household have woken up; or later, after the kids are at school; or before you go to bed at night. The point is to have minimal interruptions, so you can really pray. Consciously and with full attention, make the Sign of the Cross. Watch your right hand as it moves to your forehead, chest, and each shoulder. Now press your palms together, paying attention as you do so. Breathe in and breathe out, noticing how good it feels each time. Become aware of your chest as it rises and falls. Feel yourself relaxing as the muscles release the tension you've been carrying.

Now notice how each breath you take is an occasion of trust. As air fills your lungs, delight in it and embrace the opportunity to experience a moment such as this! Yet there is never a hesitation, never a thought that you should freeze the moment and not move on. You do not say, "I will keep this breath of air in my chest forever." No, you breathe out and trust God as one moment changes into another. You realize that the out breath is necessary so that a new breath can be born. You trust in God and his goodness every time you breathe!

God has given us many signs that we should trust in him and not fear the future. A caterpillar manifests this when it trusts enough to change into a butterfly. We welcome each dawn after a long night. As you pray, sink deeply into such reminders. Ask

God to show you how to trust him. Think of everything you would miss if you did not trust enough to embrace the light of each new day that God brings.

The ultimate sign of trust in God can be found in the Gospels. On the cross, Jesus trusts God enough to utter the words, "Father, into your hands I commend my spirit" (Luke 23:46).

Facing the unknowns in your child's life as he or she transitions into adulthood is not an easy thing to do. We must learn to trust God and hand these changes over to him. Prayer gives us the perspective, peace, and courage to do just that.

Questions

1. What were the important rites of passage in your life? Do you think your child's experiences of these rites of passage will be the same or different from yours? How does this make you feel?

2. What fears and dreams do you have about your child's current or future experience with employment? How can St. Joseph help?

3. What aspects of your child's future keep you awake at night? In what ways can prayer help you generate trust in God's plan?

Paying Attention
Is One Way to Pray

The meditation in this chapter, where we sit and focus on our breathing in order to cultivate trust in God, is an example of how paying attention to what's going on in our mind and body can become a powerful way to pray. We start by paying attention to our breathing, the feel of each inhale and exhale. Attention to the act of breathing tends to still the mind, slowing down the chaos and jumble of thoughts, so we can see with greater clarity what is happening at the moment.

Prayer helps us discover that change is inherent in our lives. Our thoughts and feelings come and go. We must allow ourselves to let go of one moment in order to embrace the next moment. We learn to trust this flow of conscious experience and embrace it as a gift from God, as we are grounded in his presence.

Father, teach us to enjoy the changing seasons of our children's lives. Help us support them as they walk through the rites of passage into adulthood. Help our children discover how to be the unique persons you want them to be. Allow us to share in their progress and accomplishments.

If at times we feel this as bittersweet, allow us to move through our sadness into the great mystery that suffering and joy are tightly bound to one another. Teach us to honor both suffering and joy. Let us praise you for the great gift you have given us in our children.

May our children learn to take risks, and may we accept the necessity that they do so. Whether this be going to college or entering the work world, may they succeed to the best of their ability. May our children with special needs find meaningful employment; may they be productive and happy. May their adult years be fruitful and safe.

Help us, O Lord, with the many decisions that we need to make. Help us decide about guardianship, living arrangements, day programs, financial planning, and other issues. Help us lay a firm foundation for the care and prospering of our child.

Help us cultivate trust in you and your divine providence. Help us give our cares to you and know that you will provide. May we never fear change but see each new challenge as an opportunity to trust in you.

CHAPTER TEN

Amazing Grace

A newborn baby has an amazing way of bringing immediate joy into your life. Our younger daughter, Shannon, came into the world hours after the terrorist attack on the World Trade Center in 2001. Our nation was in shock and glued to their televisions. The images of twisted steel and smoke were everywhere. But when we held Shannon in our arms, we felt God's grace and goodness. We were immediately renewed.

Babies have a way of doing that. They are true gifts from God.

As Catholics, we wanted our children to know God deeply in the sacraments and in prayer. Many parents share this desire. Shortly after their baby is born, they start to plan for the christening, when the child will be formally initiated as a member of the Church family. They look forward to the days when they will celebrate First Holy Communion, confirmation, and maybe matrimony or holy orders.

Family members assure new parents that time will go by quickly, that before they know it, their baby will grow up. The years did go by quickly for our family. Around the time of Shannon's birth, we were standing in the church with our eldest child, Brendan, to celebrate his First Holy Communion. Two years later, our son Colin made his sacrament.

We expected Danielle to follow her brothers and make her First Communion in the same way. However, her autism meant she needed a specialized curriculum and teaching style. Traditional catechism classes were not practical for her, due to her inability to speak, read, or use a textbook. She could not sit at a desk in a classroom and attend to a traditional lesson or lecture.

There was a path to teaching Danielle about the faith. We knew it, and we were determined to discover it. We wanted all of our children to receive the sacraments. They are perhaps the most tangible way that we experience God in our lives.

You may question whether it is possible for your child to make their First Holy Communion and receive the Sacraments of Reconciliation and Confirmation. We questioned this too. However, we prayed fervently for it, because we knew Danielle would benefit from the sacraments. We knew she would receive God's grace through them.

Where to Start

Start by praying that your pastor and director of religious education have a program that will meet your child's needs. What exactly do you need? Will your child have difficulty attending classes? Does he or she have trouble communicating? Is physical access a problem?

When it comes to receiving Holy Communion, are there issues related to swallowing the host? Is attention a problem? That is, do you find your child squirming under the kneelers during Mass, trying to make an escape, or splashing in the holy water font? Perhaps you worry that your child will make loud squealing noises during inopportune moments of the liturgy. All of these concerns can become bases for your prayer petitions.

These are very real problems that parents of children with special needs deal with. You can see why going to Mass as a family is stressful and anxiety producing. We valued church attendance and didn't want Danielle to miss out on one of the main ways we learn about and experience God. But at the same time, we were concerned that she might disrupt what should be a prayerful environment.

We persisted in going to Mass as a family. Some weeks were better than others. In the beginning, Danielle did not last in church for long. We took turns, one of us remaining in the pew with our other three children while the other took Danielle to the back of church. There were times when we thought that Danielle would not be able to make her First Holy Communion. Her behaviors were quite challenging, especially her inability to sit appropriately at Mass. But as weeks turned into months and even years, Danielle's tolerance for the Mass improved.

We prayed that Danielle's behavior would not impede her learning or her ability to participate in her religious education. Shortly before her eighth birthday, we were overjoyed when she made her First Holy Communion, preceded by the Sacrament of Reconciliation. A few years later, she was confirmed.

Danielle's sacramental preparation was a team effort. We worked hand in hand with our parish. We are grateful that we persisted, even though we didn't have a clear map of the road ahead.

If your child is like Danielle, then you may need to find a very specific approach to religious education and saramental preparation. We know how important it is for parents to persist, even if others say that education in the faith isn't possible or necessary. We prayed, and others prayed for us. Trust your own instinct, pray often, visualize success, and receive the fruits of your prayers.

Visualizing Success

Prayer is a chance to draw close to God and align your will to the divine. One way to do this is to be visual in your prayer life, less focused on words and argument. This can allow you to sync your soul's desires, hopes, and dreams with the will of God. It can help you manifest God's will in your life and in the world, so that you can truly say, "Thy will be done, on earth as it is in heaven."

As you look for ways to prepare your child for the sacraments, visualize a successful outcome. In prayer, picture what you would like to see. Close your eyes, and imagine your son or daughter standing in line for Communion. Smile, and allow the muscles of your face to relax. See your child reach up with one hand under the other, as the priest, deacon, or extraordinary minister places the host in their hands. Visualize your child consuming the host and making the Sign of the Cross reverently, then returning to the pew to kneel in prayer. See your child calm and happy in the pew. Visualize this when you wake up in the morning and before you go to bed at night.

You can add other scenarios you'd like to see. These might include visualizing your child participating in religious education classes, at church or at home, or sitting through Mass from start to finish. You can visualize meeting with the pastor of your church and with the local director of religious education to discuss the proper supports and modifications your child might need.

When you do this enough, much of the anxiety and fear regarding your child's sacramental preparation will disappear. You will feel more at peace and less stressed. You will trust God more, allowing him to handle the details. You will see a path unfold ahead of you, roadblocks cleared, and difficulties overcome.

Persistence

We've learned that persistence is essential when it comes to laying the groundwork for your child's spiritual development. You've got to stick with it when things get tough, or you won't succeed. The process can be hard, especially if your child has trouble sitting through Mass or lacks the verbal and cognitive skill set to attend traditional religious education classes. You have to have persistence, or you will be tempted to throw in the towel before the bell rings.

Persistence is crucial when it comes to prayer as well. So often we turn to God for help with our problems, but we don't want to put in the interior work that is necessary to develop a strong prayer life. God has so much for us when we draw near to him in prayer.

Jesus promises that if we are persistent in our prayer, then we will find favor with our heavenly Father. His parable of the persistent widow assures us of this:

> Then Jesus told them a parable about their need to pray always and not to lose heart. He said, "In a certain city there was a judge who neither feared God nor had respect for people. In that city there was a widow who kept coming to him and saying, 'Grant me justice against my opponent.' For a while he refused; but later he said to himself, 'Though I have no fear of God and no respect for anyone, yet because this widow keeps bothering me, I will grant her justice, so that she may not wear

me out by continually coming.'" And the Lord said, "Listen to what the unjust judge says. And will not God grant justice to his chosen ones who cry to him day and night? Will he delay long in helping them?" (Luke 18:1-7)

It's important to remember that this invitation to pray persistently pertains to our children with special needs. Their ability to pray—both during formal liturgical activities like the Mass and on private occasions—is developed by persistent practice. Your job is to show your child that prayer is a part of life and is available to him or her on a regular basis.

Jesus told us the parable of the persistent widow for a reason: that we would develop the habit of persistent prayer and pass this on to our children. It's time for us to trust that his words are true and put them into action.

It has been ten years since Danielle received her First Holy Communion. In that time, she has learned to sit through Mass. She follows along with a picture missal, she is reverent, she receives the Eucharist, she extends her hand for the sign of peace, and she blesses herself. On Sunday mornings, she requests going to Mass and looks forward to it. Her participation now at Mass is better than we ever dreamed possible.

Danielle has truly received graces from the sacraments to follow a Christian life. Her spiritual development has surprised us and has led to improvements in every area of her life. She is content and genuinely happy. We have heard her, on her communication machine, pressing icons to say prayers and make the Sign of the Cross. We believe she is talking to God. We believe she understands that God is there for her when she needs him.

Questions

1. What do you hope for when it comes to your child's religious education? How do you picture your child's relationship with God in prayer and the sacraments?
2. Is it hard for you to attend Mass together as a family? If so, what could you include in your prayer to make it easier?
3. What persistent prayer have you been bringing to God? How can you visualize success, knowing that God values your persistent efforts?

Attending Mass
Is One Way to Pray

The Mass is the central prayer experience of the Church. It is where the people of God gather to worship in word and sacrament. In the Mass, we realize that we are not individuals in isolation but a community. When we participate in this holy and living sacrifice, we move from the profane and historical into the sacred and eternal. We become active participants in the life, death, and resurrection of Our Lord Jesus Christ. Like the two disciples on the road to Emmaus, we recognize Jesus in the breaking of the bread. In the Mass, we experience the mystery of faith.

Praying the Mass means that we maintain due reverence and attention. Like Moses on Mount Sinai, we are on holy ground. When we bless ourselves with holy water, we can turn our full attention to the movement of our hand as it traces the Sign of the Cross. Likewise, when we press the palms of our hands together, we can feel ourselves praying. When we stand and kneel, we can do so with full awareness.

As we speak and sing our parts of each prayer and song, let us speak and sing from the heart. In receiving the Body and Blood of Christ, let us embrace his life, death, and resurrection as it is being lived out this very moment. Let us recognize that we are in full communion with God and each other.

Dear Lord, you have planted in each of our souls the desire and ability to know you and draw near to you. You have provided us with the gifts of sacrament, liturgy, and prayer, so that we who long for your presence may experience you in deeper and deeper ways. Help all of us learn to partake of these gifts and make them regular and cherished parts of our lives.

May our children with special needs access these gifts fully. May they learn to attend church and participate in religious education. Grant that they develop reverential behaviors, tolerance, and appreciation for the Mass. May they join with us and with the whole Church as we honor and celebrate your great love for us in the Blessed Sacrament.

Help us persevere in our prayer and visualize success, so that we might stay strong in the faith and overcome any obstacles that arise. Help us show our children the vital and important part that prayer plays in our life. Help us model and teach its availability to them in every situation.

Lord, may all our children grow in the Spirit and breathe deeply of your love!

Chapter Eleven

Praying for Joy and Happiness

Parents of children with special needs want their children to be happy. This is a desire that they share with every parent. Sometimes disabilities create many challenges in life, both for the child and for the parent, and happiness can seem elusive. We can lose our sense of joy and even lapse into depression.

It took years for Danielle to be able to communicate emotions on her electronic speech machine. It always makes us smile now when she says, "I feel good; I feel happy." Likewise we feel concerned if she says, "I feel bad." But that ability to communicate her emotions was a long time in the making.

Danielle didn't seem to understand the meaning of emotions. Of course, she was feeling many emotions, but she lacked the vocabulary to express what she was feeling. As a result, she acted out her anger or her pain, or she was just plain giddy. We are not clear as to how Danielle learned to distinguish emotions—maybe by divine intervention, the fruit of prayer.

In the Gospels, Jesus tells us that he came so we may have life and have it abundantly (John 10:10). He extends his joy to all of us. It is important to remember that God wants us to be happy. It is equally important to realize that happiness doesn't come because everything that happens is good or what we want. Instead happiness comes from embracing all of life's ups and downs with a joyous heart.

For children with special needs, cultivating happiness can be hard. Children with sensory integration difficulties can find normal sounds disturbing and even painful. When Danielle was a young child, she was very bothered by the sounds of a vacuum cleaner, a fire alarm, and a can opener. Any of these sounds would have her crying uncontrollably, long after the sound had ceased. It got to the point that we only vacuumed when she was outside or at school. We used to take the electric can opener out to the porch, plug it in, and open the can there.

If there was a fire drill at school, Danielle became so upset that she had to come home early. It would be days before she would get on the school bus. This was traumatic for Danielle and heartbreaking for us.

No one wants to see their child distraught, especially over something as simple as a can opener or vacuum cleaner. Danielle's difficulty with sounds lasted for several years, and they made it difficult for her to be joyful. She didn't know when these sounds were going to come; they were unpredictable for her. Eventually her teachers and therapists were able to desensitize her. She still holds her ears when a fire alarm or a buzzer at a sporting event sounds, but none of these noises are as intensely painful as they were.

We are fortunate that Danielle has become a happy child who is full of energy. People tell us how wonderful it is to see her smiling, laughing, and having fun. We see her radiating joy when she figure skates at Special Olympics and when she listens to music while bouncing on her physio-ball. She is happy to be with us at the supermarket. It gives us great delight to see her enjoying life and spreading this joy to the people she meets.

Joy can become your child's dominant emotion. Prayer gives us the opportunity to cultivate a joyous spirit.

Cultivating Joy with Psalm 126

As we mentioned before, the psalms can be a tremendous resource as we strive to deepen our prayer life. When praying the psalms, the words seem to rise from wellsprings within us. They express our hopes and fears, our longings, and our reliance on God for true happiness. The psalms are like a treasure trove to which we can turn again and again to renew and refresh our hearts.

Psalm 126 is a prayer to God to restore our joy. The psalmist begins by remembering the joy and laughter of the Hebrews who returned to the land of Zion from captivity in Egypt. The Lord had done great things for them. But after a time, changing fortunes led to tears and sorrow.

> When the LORD restored the fortunes of Zion,
>> we were like those who dream.
>
> Then our mouth was filled with laughter,
>> and our tongue with shouts of joy;
>
> then it was said among the nations,
>> "The LORD has done great things for them."
>
> The LORD has done great things for us,
>> and we rejoiced.

> Restore our fortunes, O LORD,
>> like the watercourses in the Negeb.
>
> May those who sow in tears
>> reap with shouts of joy.
>
> Those who go out weeping,
>> bearing the seed for sowing,

shall come home with shouts of joy,
> carrying their sheaves.

This beautiful song rises to God from the hearts of his people, who long for the joy they once knew. Parents of children with special needs can relate to this. Many of us look at our lives and discover that the stresses of parenting a child with a severe disability seem to take the joy out of life. This is especially true when our children are young, and we are grappling with the changes that disability brings to a home. We can be tempted to divide our lives into before and after the disability. When this happens, we can turn to God and ask him to return the joy we seem to have lost.

Psalm 126 doesn't end in sorrow. Instead it transforms hearts and leads to joy. To appreciate this better, it's helpful to discuss some of the imagery.

The psalmist prays,

Restore our fortunes, O Lord,
> like the watercourses in the Negeb.
May those who sow in tears
> reap with shouts of joy.

The Negeb is a region in southern Israel near the Sinai Peninsula. It was and still is a very dry land. The inhabitants constructed an elaborate series of conduits, to collect the sparse rainfall and channel it to the fields. Thus they turned the desert into prosperous farmland. The psalmist prays that like the waters in the Negeb, our tears may reap an abundant harvest of joy.

We can pray this psalm with confidence, knowing that our tears contain the seed of new grain. We know that God will direct his life-giving waters to sustain us and fill us with joy.

The Stations of the Cross

The cross sits as a great paradox and mystery at the heart of our Christian faith. Although it represents the tremendous suffering that Jesus endured on Calvary, it is at the same time a symbol of God's great love for us and a necessary prelude to resurrection and victory over death. Praying the Stations of the Cross can help us appreciate this great mystery and the promise of new life given us in Christ Jesus.

Recently we had the opportunity to participate in a retreat for families of children with special needs. We were led through the wooded grounds of the retreat house to each of the fourteen stations, which had been constructed by a previous group of retreatants out of tree limbs, stones, and other items found on the site. Our somber procession stopped by each station to reflect and pray. We were greatly affected by the rough and abstract sculptures.

Fr. Mike, who was leading the retreat, read a meditation at each station that helped us grapple with its meaning. Each station ended with the same hauntingly beautiful refrain: "We adore thee, O Christ, and we bless thee, because by thy holy cross, thou hast redeemed the world."

As we finished the fourteenth and final station and turned back toward the retreat house, a change seemed to have taken place. Our steps were lighter, our shoulders no longer quite so hunched. Our hearts, grim and burdened just moments before, had lightened too. There was now room for joy to enter in.

You don't have to go on retreat to pray the Stations of the Cross, though we found this very beneficial. You can pray the stations at your local parish. Usually they appear as paintings or sculptures on the inside walls of the church. You can pray alone, standing at each station and reflecting on the event depicted, or more commonly as part of a formal Lenten prayer service. You can even find prayers for each station on the Internet.

However you choose to pray them, the Stations of the Cross can help you make sense out of the mystery of the cross. They can lead you to a place where joy can enter in.

Everyday Miracles

About a month ago, we were surprised to find a school assignment that our younger daughter, Shannon, had done. She produced a video about who she considered to be a real-life hero. She picked Danielle. "If not for her, I would probably look at the world a lot differently, and I would take many things for granted, like the fact that I can speak. Danielle is an inspiration to many. She shows that you can overcome the hardest of obstacles, even when you have a disability."

We were filled with joy to know that Shannon had derived so much inspiration and insight from her sister. It is not always easy to be the sibling of a child with autism. It is downright hard at times!

As special needs parents, we have learned to see the miracles in everyday life. We were struck with two miracles in Shannon's video. One was the recognition that gifts like speech are not given to everyone and should not be taken for granted. The other miracle was that Danielle is a hero in Shannon's eyes, that Shannon sees her sister's struggles as heroic and recognizes the grace operating in Danielle's life.

There have been times when we have been tempted to divide our lives into before our child's disability and after. We might lament that the joy we knew before is a thing of the past. Shannon turned this on its head in her video. She made it clear that our disabled child has been a true gift and source of joy. Danielle, by being exactly who she is, inspires us with her heroism and grace. We realized that happiness is available to us here and now when we value the gift that God has given us.

Questions

1. What things fill you with joy? What fills your child's heart with joy?
2. Do you ever fall into feelings of sadness or depression? What do you say to God to help you through these feelings? What does your dialogue with God look like today?
3. How has your child been a true gift and source of joy in your life?

Going on Retreat
Is One Way to Pray

Making a formal retreat is an excellent way to break through spiritual malaise and emotional challenges. Just getting away, even if only for a day or two, can yield a new perspective and focus. Working in groups with a specific structure and set of prayer activities can be a powerful boost to your faith.

There probably are retreats that fit your particular spiritual needs and schedule. You might attend a retreat for parents and families of children with special needs or one that deals with a specific spiritual approach or tradition, such as Ignatian and Franciscan. You can find information on retreats at your local parish and on the Internet.

Praying for Joy and Happiness

God, our loving Father, we come to you in need of joy. You have created us in your image and likeness, and you have blessed us with a wide range of emotions. Help our sons and daughters with special needs learn to express what they are feeling. Let us support and guide them toward joy. May they share with us the happiness that comes from knowing you; may they experience the inner joy that you plant in the hearts of your children.

Help our child tolerate sounds, touching, smells, and other sensory input that may be troubling to them. Grant to our children happy temperaments and the ability to return to joy quickly after disturbances.

Help us discover your joy as well. May we rely on you, knowing that happiness comes not because everything is pleasurable and good but rather when, with a prayerful spirit, we fully embrace the life you have given us, with all its ups and downs. When we find this difficult and feel cracked and dry like the desert, send your living waters to flow through us. Flood us as you do the watercourses of the Negeb, that we may bring forth an abundant harvest of joy.

May we learn to see our children as inspiring and heroic. May we draw strength as they overcome obstacles, and may we support them in their struggles. Help us embrace them, as together we grow in happiness, safe in your arms, O Lord! Help us know and celebrate the gift you have given us.

CHAPTER TWELVE

Celebrating the Gift

Riding a rollercoaster can be a memorable experience. There are times when you are up at the top, with a view to end all views, only to find yourself in the next instant rushing downward, with your heart in the back of your throat. True lovers of rollercoasters know that there comes a point when you throw your arms up over your head in sheer exhilaration and joy, celebrating the ride. A rollercoaster ride is scary, it is exciting, and sometimes it makes you queasy. It is never dull.

Parenting a child with special needs is a lot like riding a rollercoaster. Prayer helps us through each of the stages: the heights, the drops, and the exhilaration. Prayer allows us to appreciate and find meaning in the experience.

This book began with the story of our family's visit to the shrine of Padre Pio. Quite a few years have passed since that trip. We've seen a lot of ups and downs.

When we started our autism journey, our hope was for a cure for our daughter. We prayed fervently that the autism diagnosis would go into our back pocket. We wanted the struggle to be short, something we could forget and never worry about again. That was our thinking; it was not God's.

We now know that God intends all his children to be seen as special gifts. Each has been uniquely created in the image and likeness of God, our loving Father. This is as true of children with special needs as of any of God's children.

We have learned to recognize the divine image in Danielle and in other special needs children we have met. A strong prayer life has brought us to this point more easily than we would have come otherwise. Prayer allows us to celebrate the gift that God has given our family.

Something else we have learned: when children with special needs struggle to overcome their many challenges, their parents struggle along with them, in the depths of their souls. When parents are open to the grace of God, their hopes and dreams and fears rise up like incense as the sincerest form of prayer.

At times it is hard to trust that these prayers are heard, but don't focus on that. Just continue to feel whatever emotions you feel as you long for your child's success. God will take care of the rest. Never give up hope. Pray, pray without ceasing. Or as St. Padre Pio said, "Pray, hope, and don't worry."

We don't know where our family would be without prayer. It has become the foundation for our life, as we struggle with life's challenges and pursue authentic and loving relationships with God, ourselves, and others. In all true and loving relationships, there is speaking and listening, waiting and hoping, longing and celebration, and most importantly, a deep embrace between lover and beloved. Prayer contains all of these elements: It unites us with the heart of God. It strengthens our family and allows us to discover and embrace the life God has for us. Prayer has given us perspective and taught us to value and celebrate life.

She Is Talking to God

For Danielle, learning to pray was a long process. When she was young, her attention span was short, and her impulsivity was high, making it difficult for her to concentrate and even understand the concept of quiet and centering oneself. Little by little, her ability to attend church reverently improved, and Mass attendance became a regular part of her life. She has learned to sit quietly in church before Mass starts and after receiving Communion.

Part of our family's routine is to always say grace before meals. For years we had to provide a hand-over-hand prompt for Danielle to bless herself and then wait for the grace to be finished before she ate. Over time Danielle became accustomed to this routine, and now she blesses herself as soon as she hears grace begin.

Danielle's tolerance and understanding of prayerful silence is not limited to grace before meals. We believe she talks to God and listens to him as well. Her more mature, calm demeanor has taken a lot of the autism chaos out of our family life. This has spilled over into other parts of our lives.

A parent looks forward to the day when some of the chaos of young, energetic children will subside and they learn to regulate themselves independently. Life will not be so loud. Parents of children with special needs may wonder if that day will ever arrive. We believe that family prayer has sped up this process for Danielle. She now has the typical teen ability to appreciate calmness and solitude.

Obviously, life is not perfect. There are times when things get hard for us, when it seems as if we are going over Niagara Falls in a barrel. But those times are fewer now. Prayer sustains us, and we always know that we will hit calmer water before long.

Appreciating the Present, Looking Forward to the Future

One piece of advice we'd like to offer to other parents of children with special needs, especially those with younger children, is to find ways to appreciate the present moment. This is one of the more valuable things we are learning to do. It's very easy to become focused on the negative and painful parts of our lives and to miss all the good things that are happening.

It's natural to try to escape difficulties we are going through. We may find ourselves wishing them away. But this won't lead to happiness. In fact, it can make you miserable. True happiness comes from allowing yourself to experience life and appreciate the present as it unfolds, with both joy and sorrow. Otherwise you'll wake up one morning and wonder where your life went and how you could have missed it.

We are learning that a deep and abiding appreciation of the present moment allows us to stay spiritually grounded. We aim to see things from the vantage point of faith. This gives us a panoramic view and empowers us to take a deep breath and look forward to the future.

Prayer is not about escaping your present circumstances but about learning to trust. We trust that, no matter what happens, we will get through. This is so important. We encourage you to pray. You will find yourself transformed by the presence and power of God in your life.

Wonderfully Made

Most parents of special needs children have at some point questioned God as to why their child has to face such struggles. No human being knows the answer to that question; but God, the author of all life, knows it. We might catch glimpses of the answer in the openhearted reactions of others to our children. We know that Danielle has had a profound effect on many people—including her siblings, other family members, therapists, teachers, doctors, and even total strangers.

We know that we and our children have greater empathy and compassion toward people with disabilities because of Danielle. We have learned to trust that Danielle's autism and her inability to speak are part of God's plan. When people meet her and are affected by her, that is part of God's plan too. Danielle and all individuals with special needs are, as the Book of Psalms proclaims, *wonderfully made* (Psalm 139).

Of course, staying spiritually grounded and having faith is easier said than done. When you are dealing with a medical crisis or an emotional meltdown, fighting for insurance approval or for school services, you may want to give up. You must believe that you will be successful in your efforts and that your heartfelt prayers will be heard.

As in the famous childhood story *The Little Engine That Could*, you need to draw from deep within yourself the strength to persist. In this story, the little train engine is climbing up a mountain with a heavy load. He does not feel confident at first, but as the trip continues and the terrain gets steeper, he builds his confidence by chanting over and over, "I think I can. I think I can."

The important thing to take away from this story is the need to develop confidence that our prayers will be heard. We must believe that miracles can and do happen and that God the Father is guiding us in our struggles. Even if we do not feel confident, the very act of praying will generate the energy that we need for success.

The Bible tells us that with God, all things are possible (see Genesis 18:14; Luke 1:37, for example). Jesus teaches us, in the parable of the mustard seed, that even if our faith is tiny, it can move mountains (Matthew 17:20). Knowing this, we can be confident that our prayers will be heard.

The LORD is near to all who call upon him,
to all who call upon him in truth. (Psalm 145:18)

Heavenly Father, you are the author of all things, and you alone know the answers to the great mysteries of your creation. You have given each of us life and filled us with the capacity to experience joys and sorrows, thrills and exhilarations, fears and longings. You have taught us to love and honor your sacred presence. Help us appreciate and find meaning in our lives.

Help us to love and appreciate our sons and daughters and to recognize your image and likeness in them. May we know that all our children are gifts and that each has something unique and valuable to teach us. Each has a meaning and purpose to share with us. Help us love them, Lord! Help us cherish and celebrate them for the gifts that they are!

Dear God, help our children overcome their burdens, and help us join them in their struggles! May we present ourselves to you in sincere prayer, open to grace. May our hearts burn with zeal on their behalf!

There is much we want to know, Lord. We want to know why there are so many struggles, when things will get better, and why you chose us to be parents of a child with special needs. We bring our questions to you, Lord, knowing that we may have to find answers in your silence.

We trust you with all our hearts, as we speak and listen, wait and hope, long for and celebrate. We embrace life with all its mystery. We allow you, O God, to take care of the rest!

We pray, dear God, that you will allow us to appreciate the good things all around us and to recognize the present moment as an opportunity to see things from the vantage point of faith. May we know the strength that comes from trusting that our children are gifts from you, that they are wonderfully made, and that we will be touched and made better by their presence.

Lord, take our faith, tiny as a mustard seed, and transform it with your love, that it may move mountains!

the WORD among us ®
The *Spirit* of Catholic Living

This book was published by The Word Among Us. Since 1981, The Word Among Us has been answering the call of the Second Vatican Council to help Catholic laypeople encounter Christ in the Scriptures.

The name of our company comes from the prologue to the Gospel of John and reflects the vision and purpose of all of our publications: to be an instrument of the Spirit, whose desire is to manifest Jesus' presence in and to the children of God. In this way, we hope to contribute to the Church's ongoing mission of proclaiming the gospel to the world so that all people would know the love and mercy of our Lord and grow ever more deeply in love with him.

Our monthly devotional magazine, *The Word Among Us*, features medi-tations on the daily and Sunday Mass readings, and currently reaches more than one million Catholics in North America and another half million Catholics in one hundred countries around the world. Our book division, The Word Among Us Press, publishes numerous books, Bible studies, and pamphlets that help Catholics grow in their faith.

To learn more about who we are and what we publish, log on to our website at www.wau.org. There you will find a variety of Catholic resources that will help you grow in your faith.

Embrace His Word, Listen to God . . .

Printed in Great Britain
by Amazon

37699031R00079